AF594164

POW-WOW

and other Yakima Indian traditions

Helen Willard

POW-WOW

and other Yakima Indian traditions

Text and photos by Helen Willard

Roza Run Publishing Company
Rt. 4, Box 4685
Prosser, Washington 99350

First edition

December, 1990

Text and photos by Helen Willard

Cover design and text by Nancy Lewis

Cover photo: Dancing Man....Bryce (Brycene) Neaman
now curator Yakima Nation Cultural Heritage Museum

Printed in the United States of America

ISBN #: 0-9627594-0-6 Soft cover
0-9627594-1-4 Hard cover

Roza Run Publishing Company
Rt. 4, Box 4685
Prosser, Washington 99350

This book is dedicated to my Indian friends.

**Ike (Isaac) Smartlowit,
drum maker.**
(Page 19)

"Come join with us. Then you can tell your grandchildren you danced with the Indians...."
(Page 50)

Nettie Shawaway. A Warm Springs, married to a Yakima, is active in Tinowit Pow-wow, arts and crafts club and other community affairs. She may give the invocation, in song, at Tinowit. (Page 74)

Contents

In lists of the three staple foods of the early day Yakimas, salmon usually comes first followed by wild plants and then wild game. The Yakimas followed the salmon runs up the rivers and streams migrating to several fish "traps" or falls. One of their favorite was Tap-tut, Prosser Falls. Families came and set up their teepees. The men dip-netted the wily fish and the women dressed them out and hung them on drying racks which were placed around slow-burning fires. While some of the salmon was eaten fresh, most of it was prepared for future use. The Yakimas practice this method of fishing in a few places today.

Jim Shock
(Page 104)

ACKNOWLEDGEMENTS

My thanks to.....

First of all to the late Richard Gay, publisher of the *Prosser Record Bulletin* who urged me to pursue a writing career.

To Don Carter and Lenore Donaldson who edited my features at PRB.

To friend and author, Mary Sclick, who introduced me to the Indian People.

To my good friend, neighbor and sculptor, Nancy Lewis who encouraged me to publish my collection of Indian stories and with her artistic eye helped me numerous times.

To the Benton Rural Electric Association staff who asked me to write People stories for their publication *RURALITE.*

To the late Dixie Koenig, The Bookmark, who helped me along the way. To Mary Da Corsi, The Bookmark, who provided sustenance and encouragement.

To Prosser High School teacher Joyce Bowden who used the stories in her Washington History class and suggested it would be helpful to have them altogether in book form.

To Jim Raney who made black and white prints for me almost at a moment's notice.

To Marlys and Dean Burn who walked me through this publication process so well.

To my own family who put up with me when I was dashing off to get "another story."

My many friends who have encouraged me to do this...too many to mention...THANK YOU.

Helen Willard

In ribbon dress and shawl this little pre-schooler entertains kindergarten youngsters at Wapato where she will go to school next year. (Page 54)

Introduction

In the early days, the Yakima Indians might have been considered the wealthiest people on earth....not in gold and silver, for those were only trinkets to them....but in natural resources that provided food, shelter and clothing.

The territory of the Yakimas extended from the snowy heights and forested slopes of the Cascade Mountains on the west to the sagebrush desert bordered on the north, east and south by enoche-wana, the Big River (Columbia).

In the spring they migrated to the traditional root digging grounds. Then to the rivers and streams where they followed the great salmon runs. Deer and elk and other game were hunted in the high country. Finally, just before the winter snows the fields of huckleberries that grew on the foothills of Pahto (Mt. Adams) were harvested.

The People's survival from year to year and generation to generation was assured. Their way of life was in rhythm with nature. Earth and life were sacred. The land taught material and spiritual values.

Because food was plentiful and preparation and preservation took only a part of the year, the Yakima Indians had time to develop the art of stone cutting (petroglyphs and pictographs), bone carving and basket weaving to a high degree. They used materials at hand — tules or cattails, grasses and bark. To enhance their articles they used fur, feathers, elk teeth and dyed, split porcupine quills. After the explorers came they had trade beads with which they made the designs for which they are so famous today.

The intricate designs on their baskets, soft bags, moccasins and vests were usually of natural phenomena. To a great extent the designs reflected their feelings. One method of cooking used water-tight woven baskets. Heated stones were dropped into water or other liquid in them.

They gathered for First Feasts, religious ceremonies and Pow wows to thank their Creator for their blessings and share their bounty.

Training was informal and by precept. Around the winter fire aged relatives related stories, myths and traditions to the children. They were trained to be self sufficient yet respectful to others.

In the 1700's the Yakimas acquired horses and they became skilled horsemen. The horses made possible expeditions to the plains east of the Rockies for trading and hunting.

Then came explorers by sea, the Lewis and Clark expedition, missionaries, fur traders and trappers and settlers on the land.

In 1850 the Land Donation Act was passed by Congress which encouraged easterners to come to this new land in the west. Isaac Stevens, Governor of the Washington territory and Superintendent of Indian Affairs surveyed for a railroad line to the west coast. In 1854 a Treaty Commission was appointed to deal with the Indian tribes in Washington territory.

Apparently those tribes on the western side of the mountains willingly signed the treaties to cede their land and live on reservations.

When the Yakimas were confronted with such a treaty at a General Council meeting near Walla Walla in June 1855 they reasoned: "How could they sign the treaty when they felt no ownership for the land? The Creator had given it to them as well as the salmon and other food to sustain them. How could they take money for something that was not theirs?"

They believed:

" My Mother is the earth
My Father is the Light
When I die, my body
Will return to my Mother
And my spirit to my Father."

After much persuasion, reluctantly they signed the treaty June 9. By signing the treaty they agreed to cede 15,920 square miles of their country and retain only 1,875 square miles for a reservation.

The Yakima Nation, a confederation of 14 tribes and bands was created as a result of the treaty.

Skirmishes occurred between the whites and the Indians. Some of the Indians were never corraled to the reservation but died in places other than their homeland.

Today Indians live in two worlds...that of our present day high tech and TV and that of their fathers where the rhythm of nature is followed. Some of this is possible today, some is not. Those who have recognized the importance of their heritage have made an effort to revive, cultivate and pass on their knowledge of it.

We feel privileged to know these People whose stories are on the pages of this book. All of the stories and most of the pictures have appeared in RURALITE.

Helen Willard

Five men drummed for the Mother's Day party at Toppenish. Each drum is made individually according to the requirements of each drummer. Note the various methods used in stringing the drums. The drums are also used in certain religious and other ceremonies.

Bryce Neaman is a modern man, but he draws sustenance from ancient roots. His dancing is a way to share that heritage.

DANCING MAN!

Bryce Neaman learned to dance almost as soon as he learned to walk.

Dressed in a typical outfit for little Indian boys and encouraged by his parents, he followed his older brothers and sisters onto the floor and stepped to the beat, beat, beat of the drum when his family attended feasts and pow-wows.

Then came school, and there were other things to do. About the time he was in the ninth grade, he began to realize that he was different from some of his classmates. He began "to find himself." He realized that he was an "Indian kid" with talents of his own and from a family with a culture of its own.

When the Indian Boys and Girls Club of Granger High School was formed, Bryce became a member. He found this an opportunity to learn more about the culture of his people — the songs, dances and ways of his forefathers — and an opportunity to perpetuate that culture and to provide understanding of it to others.

This took only a part of his high-school time. Bryce was a star basketball and baseball player, named the most valuable player on his team and awarded scholarships. "It pays to be an athlete when it comes to the fancy war dancing." says Bryce. "Our dances today take a lot of energy — especially with all the regalia we wear.

"Originally war dances were performed by the braves going into battle the next morning," he explains. "They were dressed in buckskin and eagle feathers. Some, like the Sioux, wore scalps from previous forays as fringe on their breechclouts. It was a pep talk to themselves, more spirited and with more meaning. Only the warriors danced, as opposed to our Inter-Tribal dancing."

This Inter-Tribal dancing has caused changes in the dance, the drums, the chants and the attire. Because some of the items —such as eagle feathers and bones — are seldom available any more, modern dancers have had to become creative in making substitutions. For example, turkey feathers are colored to resemble those of the eagle.

The first thing one notices of Bryce's regalia are the brilliant orange bustles worn on his back, neck and arms. The feathers surround beadwork of a family design, the six points denoting the six working days of the week and the circles symbolizing the Earth.

Bryce has made a number of these fancy bustles. His friends would like him to make more, but it is quite a chore. "You can get directions for making them, but nowhere in anything I've read does it tell what a mess it is — with feathers and hackles flying all over! The feathers must be counted, laid out and cut to the exact same size, glued and/or wrapped with a strong thread, hackles tied to the tip of each feather. All are attached in the right manner to a plywood or heavy plastic board to maintain the perfect shape."

It has taken Bryce eight years to assemble his colorful outfit for dancing the fancy war dances, and it would have taken much longer without the help of his mother and three aunts.

The cuffs of fringed buckskin and beadwork are traditional. The harness of a matching design is a modern accent. On his beaded belt he wears a small bag of buckskin decorated with a beaded design. The roach or head dress is constructed of porcupine guard hair and hair of the white-tailed deer. The base is of braided yarn or fine cloth. Bryce's roach is a handmade one from South Dakota. When not in use he folds it around his whistle and wraps it carefully with a length of cloth or plastic. For wearing he places two eagle feathers into sockets which allow the feathers to rock back and forth in perpetual motion during the dance. A choker worn around the neck is of bone. The headband is also a modern version with matching design.

The apron or breechclout and shoulder cover are made of a fine woolen cloth appliqued with an eagle feather design. The anklets are of angora goat from Arizona, for which Bryce traded a beaded whistle. These are popular because they swing in the dance. Low moccasins, also with matching beadwork, are worn. Bells are worn just below the knee. These are small sheep bells attached to a leather strap with sheepskin for lining to protect the leg.

To complete his attire Bryce carries a long whistle and a scarf which swings as he dances.

"Yes, it's heavy. And everything must be securely fastened, because to lose anything — even so much as a feather —disqualifies you. One time when I was in a contest at White Swan and there were only six of us left with four prizes ranging from $500 to $100, I lost a bell! Of course, this disqualified me. I'd tried to make my own bells, but right then and there I went to the saddlery."

Bryce continued his dancing while attending Utah State University, traveling about the country with a special group. "Probably my most rewarding experience was when we danced for a mentally-retarded group. They appeared so appreciative. Even more, it made us realize that other cultures have retarded children also."

Bryce danced with a group at the Speelyi-mi Arts and Crafts Show at the Yakima Indian Nation Cultural Heritage Center and in the men's fancy war dance division at the Satus Pow-Wow. While he enjoys dancing, he does not want it to become a show or commercial, but rather for understanding.

Dancing has always been a part of the Indian culture. There are marriage dances and dances at the time of birth and death. As the tribes have become intermingled with each other and with other nationalities, the dances and dress have become more elaborate and the drum and chants have increased in tempo. From the simple hop of the early days as the men tried to leave the bad things of Earth and become a part of the spiritual world, the dance has developed into ones of more movement, even with spinning and whirling.

"Each person really does his own thing as long as he follows the chant and the drum beat," comments Bryce. "Indians are competitive. They like to vie against each other. They like to be best. Contests at the pow-wows for children, teenagers, adults and elders with prizes of hundreds of dollars and/or blankets, beadwork and other choice gifts attract dancers and drummers from all over the western part of the United States."

The young people tape the music so they can practice at home and become better aware of the music and dancing of other tribes. Bryce has in his collection at least 100 tapes with several chants on each and from all parts of the country.

Bryce is at his family's home on the Satus helping his father, a disabled veteran. "One of us boys is always at home to help because our father cannot do heavy work. And he has done so much for us. He is a unique person, a Shoshone from Washakie, Utah, the first Utah Indian to receive a college degree. He worked in the health department of the Yakima Indian Agency and has helped many of our people."

Non-Indians are welcome to attend Yakima Nation festivities, with the exception of the Washat religious services.

A Neaman family design. The six points denote the six working days of the week and the circle symbolizes the earth.

Ike (Isaac) Smartlowit

DRUM MAKER

Ike (Isaac) Smartlowit spreads out his paraphernalia and starts another day's work. He's doing what he likes best — making drums. He is one of the very few, if not the only, Yakima Indian who makes these hand drums used in longhouse and Washat religious and other ceremonials.

In a soft voice, this small framed 70-year-old commences to talk about himself and his drum making.

He uses a special wood — usually birch. "It must be green and pliable so it will bend," says Ike. He works on a piece of the desired length determined by the size of the drum, until he can get the two ends together, then glues and clamps them until dry.

"This is the new way," he remarks. "We used to hold them together with sinew." When the glue is dried, Ike smooths and sands until he has a perfect round frame over which he stretches the soft deer skin. The skin is soaked — up to two weeks in colder weather — then scraped and smoothed on both sides.

"One of the secrets of making these drums is to know just how tight to stretch the skin," he states as he adjusts his hat. With a homemade needle, formed from a piece of wire that is bent together and squeezed with pliers, Ike carefully sews strips of deer hide to the frame. Excess hide is trimmed off, cut into narrow strips and crisscrossed on the back of the drum for the handle.

Immobility does not prevent Ike Smartlowit from doing the things he likes best to do — sing, drum and carve.

He finishes the drum with colorful artwork, along with feathers which hang down making it distinguished in its own way. Carefully and intricately done, it takes Ike about a week to finish a drum.

Ike works at the ceramic center in Toppenish, which is one part of the rehabilitation program of the Yakima Indian Nation Comprehensive Community Alcoholism program. This program provides work for alcoholics and those with alcohol related problems who want to change their way of life.

Ike is the only survivor of 14 children born to Nettie and George Smartlowit. He's been on crutches or in a wheelchair most of his life, but immobility has not prevented him from doing the things he likes to do —sing, drum and carve. He's also worked in the hop fields, driven truck and tractor, put up hay, cut wood and hop poles, and has crawled about the fields topping rutabagas.

He recalls the last day he walked. "I was six years old," he says. "We, my folks, were camped out where they were picking hops. It was a large camp with lots of children. My mother gave me some change and I ran to the store with the other kids to spend it. On the way back, I got a pain in my leg, and it hurt real bad. When the pain persisted, the older boys tried to carry me back to camp but finally had to call for my father.

Ike managed to get around on crutches for about two years. Then the pain hit the other leg, and for the next seven years he laid on his back in bed. The diagnosis was tuberculosis of the bone.

His brothers, sisters and cousins would come in after school and teach him to spell and read as they learned. When he was able to get about, he went to school at Tampico for three years.

Ike wanted to join the singing and drumming at the longhouse church, so he watched his elders closely and learned from them.

Traditionally, the grandparents are the storytellers who pass on the legends and history of the people. "I listened good to my grandfather, 'old Man Smartlowit'. He was one of the heroes of his time. He told about how he and other brave men hunted and run off the soldiers and white men who wanted to take over our land."

The "old Man" also told Ike how the people depended on the salmon runs which annually ascend the Columbia River and its tributaries; how they gathered and preserved roots, berries and game for food; and the ingenious ways they used the products of the land and how these gifts would forever be renewed as long as they believed in the Creator.

"When I was a small boy," he continued, "the Valley was all sagebrush. There were few farms around White Swan, but there were lots of Indian people. They all seemed old and they spoke the Indian language.

"We had no electricity. We used kerosene and wood stoves. We slept and ate on the floor. Many of the foods we eat today were not available at that time. We lived in a wooden house at Tampico, but we camped out when working, picking berries or attending Pow-Wows."

Ike recalls, too, the long houses covered with swamp grass (tule) with open fireplaces where the whole family "lived together and looked after one another."

He pauses, adjusts his hat again and his eyes twinkle as he thinks back to fishing days. "People came from all over to fish at certain places. One time when I was on a teetering scaffold near the Sunnyside Dam, holding a gaff, I fell into the turbulent water. I went under; came up and thrashed around; went down again; and I was sure I was going to die. So I just relaxed and let the swift water carry me along. I floated down the river and the current carried me over to the bank where I was able to get out."

His stories go on and on. They would fill a book.

The old drum maker is excited about getting a helper — a young nephew —not only because it will help him fill the drum orders but because he can teach someone else the techniques of this dying art. He also teaches the young people the traditional singing and drumming. Ike is also looking forward to the next celebration where he can sing and drum, just like in the days of his ancestors.

Ruth Howard's cuppin or digging tool is made of steel nowadays; her root basket was woven from hop-string by an aunt.

ROOT DIGGING

It was a gentle spring day when the Wapato Head Start youngsters, Rosemary Miller, their teachers, aides, parents and volunteer grandmothers boarded three vans for a day in the hills. They were going "root digging."

The caravan crossed Medicine Valley to Old Maid Canyon, passed the check station into the Yakima Indian Reservation and headed up the hillside. They saw wild flowers and wild horses. After several miles of desert roads, a spot was located that was ideal for "digging."

Ruth Howard, cultural teacher, had been talking to the children in their classes for several days previous to the outing about the significance of the roots.

"Roots, along with salmon, berries and game, were the mainstay of the Indians before the white man came," she told them. "Many of our people still dig and use them. But, before the general membership of the tribe goes to the hills for them, we must have a root feast. A few selected women and occasionally a few young girls go early into the hills to dig a sufficient amount of roots for the feast for all who care to come. The women who go must go willingly, and they must have no anger in their hearts.

It did not take the youngsters long to master the cuppin. They were excited when they got up a root, especially one that could be eaten raw.

"The feast is a feast of thanksgiving, a ceremony to thank the Great Spirit for providing this food for us. It is a joyous occasion. The feasts are usually held in April but it depends on the season — when the root growth begins, when the barren landscape begins to turn green in the warm spring. There are several locations on the Yakima Reservation where the feasts are held. We prefer to have an open building with a dirt floor according to our tradition," she said.

The roots that were found in the dry rocky soil this day were bitter roots, *punk u, sekou-ya* and *mumman* (approximate spelling).

Mrs. Howard showed the children each one, the foilage above the ground and the roots below. She showed them her root gathering bag which was tied around her waist. It was a gift, she said, from an aunt. It was made of hop string. In the early days the Indians picked hops each fall. They picked up the discarded string, rolled it into big balls and made baskets with it.

Mrs. Howard showed how to use the *cuppin*, the digging tool, so little soil was disturbed. "The *cuppins* are made in the blacksmith's shop of metal bent just the right way. The handle may be made of wood or bone. In the days of the Model T, a piece of the steering wheel made an ideal handle.

"The bitterroot, which grows all over the northwest, has long slender roots. It should be peeled and washed thoroughly. When it is properly prepared it turns white, otherwise it will turn red. It is dried and stored and cooked for a few minutes like potatoes, or used to thicken fish gravy. It will also freeze well in plastic containers," explained Mrs. Howard.

"The *punk u* is a little round root that can be peeled and eaten raw. If you save the string-like heads it can be hung to dry.Then is should be ground and mixed with *sekou-ya* or *mumman* to make a bread. Sometimes it is made into biscuits which we munch in the wintertime.

"Another round root, one that is all sized but is usually the largest of all, is the *sekou-ya.* It is peeled, ground, dried and used in the wintertime for mush. It is good plain or with fish.

"*Mumman* is also a white root which when dried is used like the *sekou-ya.*"

The celery had come earlier, and carrots and potatoes and a root similar to onions would be later. There are many kinds of roots in certain locations at certain times. Fences and farms have taken some of the former root digging areas.

It was not long until the older children were using *cuppin* to advantage. A few wandered off to find something more interesting, and one little fellow found throwing rocks the most fun.

When the children tired of digging it was lunchtime. Caroline Sohappy Charles brought forth sandwiches, fruit and milk from the ice chests. Then the group headed home, along the ridge of the Ahtanum. Mrs. Howard said, "We must show the little ones how to dig roots, dig them the right way because we will not always be here to do it. They must learn and carry on the old traditions or they will be lost forever."

Elana Smartlowit, hostess for the Huckleberry Feast.

Ambrose Smartlowit, host for the Huckleberry Feast, had been to the mountains the day before to pick pine cones. When roasted the tasty nuts were shelled from the cone by early arrivals. **(next page)**

HUCKLEBERRY FEAST

Tables were laden with platters of baked salmon, huge bowls of huckleberries and chokecherries, Indian carrots and potatoes, bitterroot and white pine moss sauce. There were plates of sliced tomatoes, cucumbers, cantaloupe and watermelon, store-bought doughnuts and sweet rolls, corn-on-the-cob and boiled new potatoes.

Friends and relatives had gathered at the Ambrose and Elana Smartlowit home for a First Huckleberry Feast. Majestic, snow-capped Pahto (Mt. Adams), the sacred mountain of the Yakimas, towered over Medicine Valley and the secluded ranch home of the Smartlowits, where they have lived for 40 years. A warm sun shone and a gentle breeze billowed the tall grass. The Feast was to thank the Creator for another bountiful season.

In the early days, the richest people on this continent could have been the Indians of the Northwest. Not rich in gold and silver — which to them was merely ornamental — but wealthy in those things which could be eaten, worn or used as shelter from the weather.

Because there were fish in the streams, berries and roots in the open places, and trees for their shelters, they spent only a part of the year gathering food. This left plenty of time for giving thanks to the Creator, feasting and ceremonies. The first harvesting of the products of the land — the roots and berries — and the first salmon catch were always preceded by a religious ceremony.

The Old Ones retain their customs and traditions and try to teach their progeny. And some of the young ones recognize the beauty and significance of those old ways. It is a pleasure and privilege to participate and share with them.

It had taken days, perhaps weeks, for the Smartlowits to prepare the food for so many people; there must have been 150 or more. "The public is invited to all of the Yakima Nation socials," states Smartlowit.

Pine cones, with their tasty seeds, were picked only the day before by Ambrose and his son, Sam, who lives in White Swan. They know the best places to go, when the cones are ready for picking, where the trees are not too hard to climb. The day of the Feast, the cones were placed on hot stones in a covered pit and roasted for about an hour. Ambrose and the early arrivals sat on the ground or in comfortable chairs around the pit and shelled the "nanuk" nuts.

The salmon was filleted and baked in ovens in wood burning stoves set up in a lean-to on one side of the church building.

Others filleted and chunked the salmon, which was then baked in the oven of a wood-burning stove. On top of the three ranges in a lean-to were huge pans of the bitterroot (the staple Indian food), the moss sauce that tasted somewhat like licorice and other vegetables. The young fellows, assured an adequate supply of wood, stoked the fire in the oversize sheet-iron camp stove outside, where a wash-tub full of corn was cooking.

The sounds of a tinkling bell, swung to and fro by the leader of the independent Shaker religion, brought family, friends and guests into the church building. Three long tables were set in the main room and a fourth in a small room off to one side. The leader, standing by a small table with lighted candles in the front of the room chanted prayers and songs and rang the bell as people were seated.

He sang the old songs of thanksgiving. He told how the ways of the Old Ones meant sharing with friends and worship of the One who gives food needed for the body. He mentioned that cycles of living are linked with nature, the sacredness of the Earth as well as Life on it. Land contains both material and spiritual values. Spiritual values have diminished in intensity as material values have been established.

The ceremony continued as five persons (from young to old) assisted by serving food. As they moved around the room (from right to left as the earth turns), the first one poured a sip of water into each cup. The next one placed a tiny bite of salmon on each plate, followed by one who put two chokecherries to the left of the fish. Then came one who placed two huckleberries to the left and lastly there was one pine nut.

After the water had been blessed, each one took a sip. The leader directed that the meal begin, and blessed each food before it was eaten. When this was finished — and only then — the platters of food were passed up and down the long rows of people. These dishes were placed in the center of the table. Later, hunks of delicious dried salmon were passed.

Everyone ate and ate and ate — the scrumptious salmon, juicy berries, fresh vegetables and fruits. And there was visiting among old friends and new friends, among young and old. There were babies in arms and great-grandparents. The widows sat on one side of the room and the widowers on the opposite side.

It was a colorful crowd, with the women in their hand-sewn, bright-colored wing dresses, kerchiefs and shawls, while others wore bright new clothes from the store.

The long hair of many of the older ones and a few of the young ones tells the Creator they are faithful to the ancient traditions and customs of the ancestors, to their Mother (the Earth), to their friend and provider (the Chiawana or Columbia River), and to their brother (Nasau the salmon).

The Smartlowits follow the old ways of life. "We don't need a telephone. We just go to see our friends or neighbors," says the genial host. Neither do they have electricity, although Benton Rural Electric lines run nearby. "We people stick together. We look out for each other."

The ranch nestled near the foothills of the mountain is quiet and serene much of the time. "A small creek runs most of the year, but it can be a torrent," comments Smartlowit.

Ambrose raises grain, pigs and dogs. "At one time we had 190 brood sows," he says, "but a flood about three years ago wiped out a good many. We couldn't get in to feed them. Then we had a warm spell, followed by cold weather, and a lot more bunched up and smothered."

The ranch boasts an orchard, too, with a variety of fruit trees, most more than 70 years old.

It is difficult to maintain the Culture and keep the heritage of the Old Ones in today's society. It is the hope of the Smartlowits and their friends who live in the area that their children will learn to prepare these foods, and preserve not only their traditions and legends but their special food.

Celebrations, feasts and fellowship together will help. It is also good that those outside learn and understand the true meaning of their culture.

On top of the stoves, bitterroot, moss sauce and other vegatables are cooked.

Judy Neaman, Miss Yakima Nation 1979. The baskets were made by and used by the Neaman family for gathering huckleberries and other wild foods.

It may take as long as two hours for a complete formal dressing. Judy will add otter skins to her long black braids which may reach to her knees because she lives near the water.

MISS YAKIMA NATION

Dancing is a language of movement; it is self-expressive and relaxing. And whether it be her native Indian or modern disco, Judy Neaman loves it.

Judy was crowned Miss Yakima Nation at Tinowit last June. More than 400 Indian dancers, 120 singers and 15 drummers had come with their families and friends numbering in the thousands to compete for prizes in this annual "gathering of the tribes."

Tinowit (pronounced Tin-ow-it) is an international pow-wow held at the ancient ceremonial grounds near White Swan to celebrate the Yakima Indian Nation Treaty Signing Day. It was June 9, 1885 that a treaty was signed creating the Yakima Nation — a confederation of tribes and bands — and setting aside a specific area of central Washington as a reservation.

This year a purse of S13,000 attracted outstanding dancers and drummers from as far away as Florida and New York. There were classes for tiny tots, teenagers and senior citizens in traditional and fancy dancing — shawl dances, war dances, buckskin dances and tribal exhibitions of the Snake Dance, the Shield Dance, Hoop Dance and others.

The crowning of Miss Yakima Nation and Miss Tinowit followed the grand entry, a mutual tribute of tribe to tribe and an honoring of the Yakima Nation on Treaty Day. The new Miss Yakima Nation was crowned by Trudy Pinkham, Miss Washington Birthday Celebration Queen. Her exotic beaded crown with the Yakima Nation insignia woven into the design was made by Patricia Iukes in honor of the deceased 1978 Miss Yakima Nation, Margaret Pinkham, killed in an automobile accident only a short time before and to whom the entire 1979 Tinowit was dedicated.

After the ceremony the two girls led off the first dance, followed by family, friends and guests in their brightly-colored buckskins, beads and feathers as the beat of the drums rang from rafter to rafter in the huge longhouse.

The dancing, singing, chanting, visiting and drumming continued for three days. The two young ladies distributed blankets, jackets, trophies and cash to five winners in each category of the competition.

Judy is the daughter of Mr. and Mrs. Lee Neaman of Satus. She is a graduate of Granger High School, where she received many honors. She now attends Brigham Young University, majoring in secondary education with a minor in Native American Studies.

Her mother, who works with Tribal Nutrition, is Yakima; her father is Shoshone. He is the first native American to graduate from Utah State University. A former teacher and executive director of the native American Program, he has also been involved in Public Health.

Judy's older sister Lorena, now Mrs. Tony Washines and a student at Utah State, was Miss Celilo. Brother Delford is also a student at BYU; he makes the colorful bustles worn by war dancers, an art learned from his grandfather. Brother Brycene attends USU, and younger sisters Odessa and Amy attend Granger schools.

This is not Judy's first foray into the limelight. She was Miss Indian BYU, a position from which she resigned in order to carry out her duties as Miss Yakima Nation. Because of the diverse requirements, the BYU honor was not easily won. The contestants were evaluated for poise, the ability to present themselves and their escorts, both modern and traditional talent and fashion, impromptu speaking and ability to cook native Indian foods and explain their origins. Thanks to her training at home, Judy was able to prepare Indian fried bread, salmon, huckleberry pie and several roots to the judges' satisfaction. The contest is held each year during "Indian Week" and is sponsored by the campus organization "Tribes of Many Feathers." As a member and vice president, Judy's responsibility lies in public relations.

Judy has entertained on campus and has traveled about the country with the Lamanite Generation, a BYU ethnic singing and performing group. She specializes in guitar, flute, piano and voice.

For her appearances at Indian powwows, pageants and events throughout the West — as well as community affairs closer to home — this 22-year-old selects one of eight or more costumes or dresses. Some she has made, some are loaned by relatives or friends and some are heirlooms from her grandmother.

For evening or a formal event she may choose a fringed buckskin with beaded work on the shoulders made by one of her ancestors, with footwear, leggings and beaded accessories to match.

For afternoon it may be a brilliant red jersey designed and made by herself, and decorated with appliques of eagle feathers and white buffaloes. Judy learned to sew at an early age, as have her sisters. "Our parents have seen to it that each of us girls have our own portable sewing machine so we can make our own clothes. Our parents felt that if we could sew and cook we could be more independent. Now Mom says we can sew and cook better than she does."

The beadwork is also of Judy's creation. Her designs are of her favorite colors and things — roses because they are so beautiful, eagle feathers because they are sacred, buffalo because the bison served as food. Colors range the spectrum: gay reds, oranges, purples on a white or cream background. Blue is a typical Yakima color, especially significant in religious affairs.

It may take as long as two hours for a complete formal dressing, including the braiding of her long black hair. Her braids are enhanced with otter skins which reach nearly to her knees "because we live near the water" and with beaded or shell barrettes. A neck piece — a rainbow of her own design — and conch shell earrings are selected. She carries a beaded bag loaned by a friend, a blanket given as a gift of Tinowit and an eagle feather fan received at Fort Hall. Without her beautiful beaded crown, she may wear a head band and eagle feather plume.

Judy with her parents, Mr. and Mrs. Lee Neaman who have lived on the Satus for many years.

There's much fun attached to representing her people — traveling with her mother or Nettie Shawaway as chaperone, meeting people and royalty — but there is also responsibility. Judy has studied herself to try to understand why she was chosen for this important task. She said to herself, "What do you have to offer? How can you bring out the best in others?" She tried to find out who she really is and how to teach people to look into their culture and discover who they really are.

Miss Yakima Nation will represent her people well with her dancing, her music and her beautiful clothes; with her sparkling eyes and a smile that springs warmly from within.

Her objective is the sharing of cultures, the preservation of cultures. It is bringing forth the beauty of the Yakima Nation.

Dancers come from far and near to participate in dance contests. This young fellow is ready and waiting.

This young man is practicing outside the pavilion and entertaining some small lookers on.

Each Pow-wow session is opened with a parade and serpentine. Then a prayer is sung and the flag saluted. Representatives from each local and visiting tribe are represented during the three-four day gathering.

POW-WOW!

Tin-ow-wit, the treaty pow-wow, attracts Indian dancers, drummers and singers, young and old, and those who just like pow-wows to meet old friends and make new ones.

They come in cars, campers, trailers and motor homes from all over the western United States and Canada — and this year as far away as Arkansas — to participate in memorial services, social dancing and straight and fancy dance competition and drummer contests.

Tin-ow-wit is held each year around June 9, the date in 1855 when the Yakima Nation — a confederation of 14 tribes and bands — were created, and a specific area of central Washington set aside for its reservation.

The first day of Tin-ow-wit is known as camp day. A memorial is offered for those who have "walked on" during the past year and a feast is enjoyed by everyone present. This is a time for those who have been in mourning for a loved one to reenter social activities. Another traditional ceremony is the giving of an ancestral Indian name to those who have requested or consented to it.

Miss Tin-ow-it leads out onto the floor with her princesses and family following. Then everyone who cares to joins in for the first dance.

At 6:30 each evening and at 1:30 on Saturday and Sunday, the drum roll calls the dancers. A half hour later, the colorful grand entry begins. Each participant is in his or her traditional tribal dress, following a leader from each tribe carrying a banner noting the tribe.

When all have entered the building, prayers are chanted. Elders, veterans and others may be honored, and on the first evening Miss Yakima Nation is chosen — as well as a Junior Miss and Granny Tin-ow-wit queen.

The Tin-ow-wit International Pow-wow is planned and produced through the co-operation of local families and the support of local communities. A governing board finances the annual event through mini pow-wows, bingos, raffles, fashion shows and whatever it takes to make a dollar.

Along with Tin-ow-wit pow-wow just three miles away is the All Indian Rodeo. The rodeo, three days of rough arena action, is sanctioned by the Western States Indian Rodeo Association and this year by the United Indian Rodeo Association of Montana. Other entertainment includes stick games. Concessions offer arts and craft work, Indian fry bread, huckleberry pie plus the ordinary hamburgers and pop.

Fred Ike, Jr., was chairman of the 1985 pow-wow, Patricia Ike was secretary. Elder advisors were Hazel Umtuch, Nettie Shawaway, Delores and Leander George, Betsy Redbear and Rosanna Iukes, Charles Tailfeather was master of ceremonies.

Delores George, whose family "lives for pow-wow," said this is a way to encourage Indians to preserve their traditions and culture.

Rules for the competition are strict. Their regalia must be complete and in accordance with the specific event entered. Loss of an eagle feather is grounds for automatic disqualification. Dancers must keep time with the song and drum beat, whether it be fast, crow hop, chicken dance or stop song. Each drum must have five singers. Drum hopping is not permitted.

Deanna George was named Miss Yakima Nation 1985-86, Esther Bill Grandma Tin-ow-wit and Onida Colwash Miss Tin-ow-wit. Onida is from Warm Springs, Oregon, the others from the Yakima tribe. Local winners were Tubby Thompson of Satus, fourth in men's fancy dance, and Selina Johnson of Toppenish, fourth in men's traditional dance.

There are a number of pow-wows and celebrations on the Yakima Reservation each year. Most coincide with special events or holidays. The public is always invited.

ROYALITY....

Trudy Pinkham, Miss American Indian Nation, (left) and Miss Judy Neaman, Miss Yakima Nation, represent their people well. To participate in such contests a girl must know about her Indian heritage and be able to present themselves well to the public. Both girls have participated in several other contests throughout their young career.

A young Weaseltail dancer awaits the beat of the drum, his outfit carefully put together by parents and grandparents.

An unhappy moment.....

Kenneth Scabbyrobe, teacher, Weaseltail dancers.

WEASELTAIL'S DANCERS!

Every Tuesday evening, Weaseltail Club members gather at the White Swan Community Center.

The families come with their little ones on baby boards, their youngsters and their teenagers to learn the techniques of the drummers, the chants and the dances of their forefathers or to make up new ones of their own.

The Weaseltail Club was organized in 1967 by Eagle Salatsee, Jim Weaseltail, Betty Brown, Yvonne Smith and Mae Dodd as "something for the community."

There was little to do in this small farming town on the Yakima Indian Reservation, plus the Older Ones were realizing that part of their culture was being lost and were worried about it.

At first there were only a few families from the surrounding area, but when the word got out the club pulled members from all over the reservation.

The Older Ones came to teach the younger ones, and it was fun for all. Salatsee and Weaseltail were among the first teachers. Now Kenneth Scabbyrobe, from the Blackfoot Reservation and married to Weaseltail's daughter, is president of the organization and teacher. Assisting Scabbyrobe are Burke Scown, vice president; Sandra Scown, treasurer; Vicki Swan, secretary; Elizabeth Henry, tribal representative and many others. There are some funds from the Yakima tribe, but most of the financing comes from raffles, cake walks, mini-pow-wows and such.

The group revived more than the singing and dancing; also coming back are the arts and crafts involved — the making of buckskin clothing adorned with shells, beads, feathers and fur, the bustle and the roach or headdress the young men wear.

Dancing accompanied by chanting and drumming has always been a part of the Indian culture. From the simple hop step of the early days, as the men tried to leave the bad things on Earth and become a part of the spiritual world, the dance has developed to one of more movement — even with spinning and whirling, which the youngsters love and do repeatedly. Many moons ago warriors going into battle the next morning participated in war dances with spiritual meaning. They were actually giving a pep talk to themselves.

"We have many traditional dances," explains Scabbyrobe, "like the owl dance, the rabbit dance, circle dances and shawl dances and ones for courting, marriage, birth and death.

"There is no written music. It is handed down from generation to generation. The music may sound all alike to you, but to us there are different rhythms and different pitches for the chants. The drums are tribal drums, as are the drumsticks."

The Weaseltail Club now boasts two drum groups. The Weaseltail drummers and singers are those from four to 12 years of age. Some in this group are Kenneth Scabbyrobe, Sr., director, and Elgin Scabbyrobe, Gina Talpocken, Melissa Heredia, Amo Wyman, J.C. Wyman, Frank Ross, Steve Goudy, Myron Scabbyrobe, Michelle Crow and Gaston Bill. The Black Lodge group is made up of teenagers and young men and women, some of whom are Kenneth Scabbyrobe, Jr.; Darwin Running Crane; John, Shawn and Erwin Scabbyrobe; Mike Dick and Lily Scabbyrobe.

Indians, long wanderers of the land who liked to gather for feasting and games still travel hundreds of miles now by car, camper, trailer or motor home to participate in pow-wows. Pow-wows attract children, teenagers and elders of both sexes who compete in contests for hundreds of dollars and choice gifts. The pow-wow held each year at the Pavilion south of White Swan over the Memorial Day weekend is sponsored by the Weaseltail Club.

This little girl in her ribbon dress and pants look anxiously at the dancers on the floor.

As the tribes have intermingled, dance and dress have become more elaborate. There are no more eagle feathers or bone, but creative substitutions are made. Sometimes it takes several years to assemble a complete outfit, and often with much help from parents and grandparents who put many loving thoughts into their work. They are proud when their offspring win prizes. Dancers are generally judged on dance, costume and overall appearance.

"Besides our traditional dances, the young people are making up new songs and dances of their own," comments Scabbyrobe. Electronic mediums raise the decibels and tapes record for practice at home or to get better acquainted with other tribal rhythms. The fancy war dances seen today take lots of energy, especially with all the paraphernalia the dancers wear — moccasins, leggings, bells, apron or breech clout, anklets, shoulder cover, belt, bustle, choker, harness to hold the bustle, headband, etcetera.

In preparation for the pow-wows, besides the regular Tuesday-night practice, the Weaseltail Club may have Saturday-night mini-pow-wows at which participants wear their finest. There may be a potluck supper in the basement of the much-used building, after which the people drift upstairs to visit until all are ready. Just as at the regular pow-wows, there is a grand entry with the leader carrying the colors. When all have joined in, there is a salute to the American flag and a prayer in their own language. Then the music and the dancing begin.

Although there are special dances for certain age groups, there are also some in which all ages join. Almost from the time a youngster can walk, he or she is encouraged by relatives, by watching others and by the music. The Old Ones are pleased to see the younger ones start in and carry on their traditions.

The Weaseltail and Black Watch drummers and singers perform at many functions around the Yakima Valley area and of course in pow-wows here and elsewhere.

A young Weaseltail dancer in action. Dancers, young and old, adorn themselves with beads, bones and feathers.

Pow-wows held on various holidays and on Treaty Days in June are open, and outsiders are welcome. Those participating enjoy themselves, and so will you when you see their beautiful, priceless dress, the grand entries with each tribe having its own characteristics, the beat of the drum and the dancers following.

Elsie Pistolhead was an "honored elder" at the 1990 Toppenish Pow-wow held over the 4th of July weekend. Her colorful clothing from her beaded moccasins to her woven hat were designed and made by Elsie.

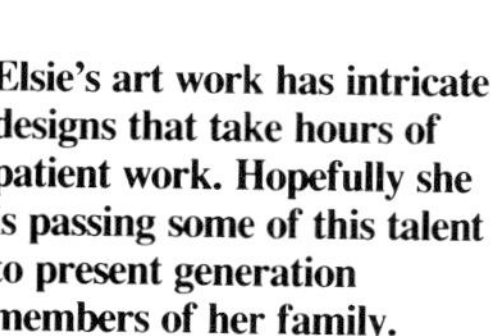

Elsie's art work has intricate designs that take hours of patient work. Hopefully she is passing some of this talent to present generation members of her family.

Elsie Pistolhead sets up her teepee at a pow-wow or a booth at an arts and crafts show and displays many beautiful pieces of handwork. Some of the bead, buckskin, tule and fur pieces she had made herself, others have come to her from the past.

SPEELYI-MI!

"Come join with us. Then you can tell your grandchildren you danced with the Indians."

This was the invitation Master of Ceremonies Bert Peters, a full-blooded Pawnee, extended to the audience at the 14th annual Speelyi-mi Indian Arts and Crafts Fair at the Yakima Convention Center last March.

Many — both Indians and non-Indians — did join the dancers when they came down from the stage to lead the round dance. The circle of dancers covered nearly half of the huge hall.

Dancing was only one part of this beautiful three-day event. The Old Ones brought their precious heirlooms of leather, beads, feathers and photographs to share with the public. The young parents brought their wee ones to compete for prizes in the baby contest (judged on personality and costume). Others offered for sale silver, turquoise, beadwork, basketry, books, sketches, paintings and Shoshone, Navaho or Yakima Indian fried bread.

The Speelyi-mi Arts and Crafts Club was formed 16 years ago by a handful of Native Americans who wished to preserve traditional Indian arts and crafts, to promote and encourage Indian people to continue their arts and to revive those craft skills which were being lost or forgotten.

Lydia Johnson (Yakima), a public health nurse, discovered many of the priceless heirlooms were being pawned or sold for a pittance because there was no understanding or regard for their value either dollarwise or as relics of a proud heritage.

Two years after the club was formed, non-Indian people were invited to join and the yearly Arts and Crafts Fair began.

"Along with the aim of encouraging Native American arts of all kinds," Johnson says, "a second goal of the Club has been to develop a greater appreciation by all people of Indian culture. To this end, we plan someday to have a comprehensive Indian Arts Center, designed by an Indian architect, which will be a credit and an asset to the Indian and non-Indian community alike."

Among the original members were the late Chief Eagle Seelatsee, a distinguished and honorable member of the Tribal Council and a leader of his people, and Alba Shawaway, a Wanapum-Yakima. Present officers of the Club are Bernice Hoptowit (Nez Perce), president; Leo Adama (Yakima), vice president; Bessie Lou Aiello (Yakima-Cayuse), secretary and Isadore Johnson (Sioux), treasurer. Aiello and Johnson were in charge of this 1978 fair.

The Fair was opened on a Friday morning with a prayer by Violet Tomaskin in the language of her Shaker religion. Indians from many tribes and as far away as Arizona and New Mexico came to participate. More than 40 tables were filled with displays of assorted hand-crafted items.

"The Old Ones had a simplicity of purpose — they do the best they could in everything they did," remarks Johnson. "They put their ALL into whatever they were making, and it shows in the finished product."

Even more important than the large display of Indian-owned heirlooms were the people in whose traditions they were made and whose keeping they belong. An example of this is Margaret Coffey, a Flathead from Spokane, who showed a feather headpiece more than 200 years old. One of only 33 in the world, it was given to her because the former owners were afraid of its powers (the bad spirits only affect the original owner).

Jessie Copenhaver, a Cheyenne, came from Montana. Caroline Miller of Lacey, Washington, had a waiting line most of the day for her Shoshone Indian fried bread. Vivacious Carrie Simpson, (Palouse-Walla Walla), drove her own pickup from Pendleton to share and to visit her friends "one more time. I come even if I break my neck!" she laughed.

Local artists Leo Adams, Nathan Olney, Bob Moldonado, Steve Gunnyon, Lana Cleveland, Lucy Eneas, LeRoy Colfax and many others helped "run the show" and/or offered their wares.

Seventy-three year old Alex Wesley, chairman of the Washington Birthday Celebration for 22 years, came with his possessions and to dance. He wore an exquisite vest with eagles and American flags that his wife, now blind, stitched for him with white and colored beads. Elsie Pistolhead, Satus, showed buckskin dresses, cedar baskets, preserved roots and root-digging tools, as her granddaughter, Linette Yallup sewed tiny beads on deerskin for a barrette for her hair.

One could watch Miles Pebeahsy fashion a ring of silver and turquoise, or buy something already made by this young silversmith. Howard Jim and Bob Moldonado promoted the Celilo village Longhouse as the artists' offerings were selected by the visitors. Bill Jame of the coastal Lummis showed how he makes baskets.

DeEtte Miller, Miss Yakima Indian Nation VIII, poised elegant in clothes made by her mother to fit her complexion and personality, mingled with the crowd and talked of her travels this year as a representative of her people at pow-wows, celebrations and parades.

Two busloads of Nespelem grade school children, most of them Colvilles, came with a display of the beadwork and necklaces they learned to make at school. Hundreds of local children were bused to the Center to view the Indian arts and crafts and watch the craftsmen at their work as part of school cultural programs. Even Home Demonstration Clubs used the Fair as an incentive for a day trip as part of their educational program.

Interspersed during the day were programs of music and dancing; a mini concert of gospel songs by a non-denominational group of Pawnee and Yakima tribal members; exhibition hoop and war dancing and social and/or traditional dancing led by Peters and Wesley.

More than $1,000 in prize money went to the contestants and to those who had the best displays, paintings, books and so on.

The Speelyi-mi Club is a non-profit organization that has not asked for nor received any federal, state, county or tribal funds to support its activities. Proceeds from the entry fees and admission, after expenses, will go towards an Indian Arts Center.

Lydia Johnson and Bessie Aiello, charter members of Speelyi-mi, Arts and Craft Organization were in charge of the 1978 fair.

Delores Miller Hart came to Speelyi-mi with her beautiful beaded items. The design on her large bag is from the heart....something she enjoys and loves.

With rings on her fingers and bells on her toes this little one is ready to have fun.

HEAD START

The pre-schoolers who attend Tribal Headstart learn the days of the week, colors, numbers, letters and how to share, clean up and put away, as do most Headstart children.

But these youngsters learn much more. They learn about their Indian heritage — dress, food, shelter, dances and the traditions which accompany each.

Some of the children live where Indian culture is part of their way of life. Others are more attuned to television.

In the spring, vans carry the youngsters to the mountain fields to gather roots. "We want to teach them what to dig and how to do it," says Ruth Howard. "We tell them they must learn the ways because we elders will not always be here to lead them."

A ceremony accompanies the root digging. "We must thank the Creator who put the roots here for us. Otherwise the mountains will be barren and roots will not be plentiful." Ruth also notes that one must not go to the fields feeling sad or angry. "You can't be angry when you handle food. You can't serve angered food." The children like the roots they can peel and eat right away. As they help prepare the ones to be cooked, they learn the traditional songs that are handed down from one generation to another.

Some Indian foods are served daily with the breakfast, lunch and snacks that the children get each day.

The youngsters learn to dance at an early age by going to pow-wows with their parents and grandparents. They love their colorful dresses made by mother, grandmother or aunt. The dresses may be the traditional wing dresses, buckskin, or they may be enhanced with ribbons and/or beads. Furs are woven into their braids. Each carries a purse on the belt and has a shawl about her shoulders. One may wear necklaces or turquoise or such. The boys feel good in their ribbon shirts and their bustles, bells and moccasins.

It's fun to perform for others and they do it frequently. Each year they entertain at the Yakima Valley College Indian Awareness Week, at the Speelyi-mi Arts and Crafts Show and for the primary classes at the Wapato school. Most of these children will attend the Wapato primary school when they are ready for kindergarten, so they have a view of what comes next fall and they may see some Wapato Headstart alumni when they go to entertain.

Funded by the National Headstart Indian Migrant Program at three locations — Wapato, Toppenish, and White Swan — the programs are coordinated. Besides director Rosemary Miller, there are two other certified teachers at the Wapato Headstart and several assistants. Ruth, who teaches many traditions, also teaches the Indian language. "If they do not learn it," she says, "it will be lost forever."

"The Indians are walking in two worlds," explains Rosemary, a graduate of Eastern Washington University. The other certified teachers are Alberta Lilly, also a graduate of EWU, and Sharron Tellakish, a graduate of Heritage College.

Three little boys in their ribbon shirts at Wapato Head Start.

Three little girls in their ribbon dresses at Wapato Head Start.

"Our goals are to promote their Indian culture so the children will be aware of their heritage," Rosemary says. "We will also hope to promote community awareness of the Indian culture and build a better understanding of it. We try to instill in the little ones a respect for their culture and a respect for other cultures."

Besides the 30 little ones who come to Headstart daily, Sharron visits 15 children in their homes once a week. These also have an opportunity to come to the center once each week. "We have two classes, but we really need more," comments Rosemary.

"It's very important for pre-schoolers to develop a sense of pride in their ability, to develop self-esteem, to be flexible. Children learn by role models, they constantly learn from their elders and learn to respect their elders."

Several of these little ones will participate in the Weaseltail Pow-wow and the Tin-ow-wit International pow-wow. They may dance in the social dances and perhaps some will even dance in the "lil' tots" contest. Some may travel with their parents to other pow-wows, which are social gatherings with dance contests, games, food and arts and crafts — another place to learn about their Indian culture.

The public is invited to the pow-wow and many other Indian events.

Kindergarten students of Wapato Primary watching a dancing exhibition.

Camp Chaparral

CAMP CHAPARRAL

High in the Mt. Adams country at Camp Chaparral, 110 fourth, fifth and sixth grade Indian children are learning basic educational skills and having a lot of fun at the same time.

As they skip and run from art class to math, from reading to science or from communications to beadwork, their sparkling eyes and shining faces reflect their feelings. Learning in this relaxed atmosphere is easy compared to regular school.

Of course there are those few who are shy and withdrawn. However, with a ratio of one adult who cares, to five students, by the end of the four-week session, generally the shy ones too, will be responsive and begin to bloom.

From the time the youngsters arrive by bus from the Valley until they leave, their days are full.

"Rising at 7 a.m., they raise the flag, then exercise on the paved ball courts finishing off with a bit of jogging," says activities director Arlen Washines.

After an 8:00 breakfast, there's just time to clean up the dormitories before classes start. The dormitories are double, flat-topped A frames, each housing 16 youngsters and two leaders.

Classes run from 8:15 until 12:10 and from 1:30 to 3:00 p.m., after which come organized activities such as basketball, baseball, volley ball, fishing and swimming in the Klickitat River.

Enthusiasm runs high for the evening team competition. The 10 teams compete in five sports activities, in music and in dancing. At the end of the session, members of the winning team receive trophies. "There's also an award for sportsmanship," says Washines.

These activities are supervised by Indian students active in extra-curricular activities at district public schools, and give the youngsters someone with whom they can identify when they return to their regular school.

Nature tours are frequent. Arnold Troeh, a Chinook and a science teacher, who has listened to the elderly and who has a desire to pass on to the young people the legends and traditions of their ancestors, teaches the student that the Indians were the first conservationists. Their philosophy was based on need, and it is "take all you need, but use every part of what you take."

When the children come to his classes, they explore the use of roots, leaves, bark, grasses and where to find the most suitable ones. They study the ways of the animals in their natural habitat.

The second session group had an exciting day when they were out looking for bear signs around the garbage dump — and found a bear!

Trips to Signal Peak where everyone climbs to the tower lookout, to Potato Hill, to Mt. Adams Lake and to Glenwood are fun learning experiences. They may even have a wiener roast before they return to camp.

Each day ends with a campfire and singing, a dance, a movie or other entertainment.

According to Mrs. Genevieve Hooper, a summer supportive education director, this program has been in effect eight years at the mountain camp.

The first one involved 40 high school boys and girls. This year there are two four-week sessions. The first was for seventh, eighth and ninth graders; the second for the younger ones. (There are also three such projects in the Valley at Satus, Toppenish and White Swan).

The need for the program was indicated when several years of educational research revealed a high drop-out rate of Indian youngsters in the district schools. This was due to a number of factors such as differences in cultures, unstable home life, bilingual background, lack of parent understanding, lack of motivation and eventually discipline problems.

Those attending the Yakima Tribal Council and Bureau of Indian Affairs supported remedial program are screened carefully. Most of those selected are two years behind grade level in one or more subjects, but express a desire to improve themselves and have parents who are most anxious for this to come about.

Adult staff members are usually teachers from local schools, most have Indian background, are not "stereotyped" or "hobbled to textbooks," but are "free swingers" who know how to get along with young people, who understand and are patient and who wish to share what might be a thrilling experience in the lives of the youngsters.

Aides are Indian college students whose first duty is to act as a bridge between student and teacher, but who are gaining valuable experience and training for his or her own field of endeavor.

Some children make as much as six to 12 months progress in reading, math or language skills during a session as shown by pre-camp and post-camp California Achievement test scores.

Far more important, however, are the social adjustments, says Camp Chaparral director, Don Goodwin. He points out changes in attitudes, leadership potential uncovered and emergence of motivation in certain ones.

Goodwin also stresses the importance of the well-balanced meals with plenty of fresh fruit, vegetables and meat eaten with a friendly group in pleasant surroundings either in the dining room or outdoors on the patio.

One effect not foreseen, but very beneficial to progress is the students feeling that this is their land, this is their program and this is done for them by their people. Every child is important and every child needs to feel some success, assert the sponsors and directors of the program. Therefore, they have provided the location, the personnel and the materials most conducive to gaining their goals of raising the educational level of the students, improving the student's attitudes toward education, making the best use of summer free time, minimizing the loss of education during the summer and stimulating interest of the young Indian in future learning. Camp Chaparral, with the beautiful creek by that same name running through the campsite, is a setting where students have never before been faced with academic failure. The youngsters are learning about their people, their environment, and reading English and learning math so necessary because the most widely accepted standards of behavior patterns of oral and written expression reflect the white, Anglo-Saxon, Protestant culture and materials used for instruction at school follow these standards and patterns.

Following are excerpts from letters written by older students after attending Camp Chaparral. The letters are on file at the Tribal office, Toppenish, Washington.

"Thank you for letting me come to camp. I like to be at Camp Chaparral because I think it is fun, because I like to go to school and learn math and reading."

"I think they should have a summer school every year. By having it every year, it will enable the students to learn more and have more skills to help the person in his future school years. During his stay at summer school it will help him or her get along with each other."

Activities are so diversified outside the classroom that each child can find something to his liking....something that may continue to be a hobby or even a profession in future years.

"...was a great help to me especially on my worst subject, English, which turned out the other way around now that I know the hard parts on punctuation, capitalization and other parts of speech."

"Here I am able to learn to really think about the importance of these simple subjects such as English, Reading and Math. I have come to realize the importance that they have in my life. From these subjects, I have gone into deeper thoughts and therefore I feel that these few weeks I've attended haven't been at all a waste of time."

"I sure like the camp because of the studying I get in Math and English. From Math, I got help in division of fractions. Now from English, I get nouns, pronouns and adverbs ... one thing is wrong, though, ... the floor in the girl's dorm has a hole so the squirrels can get in and eat all my sunflower seeds."

Winter lodge

REMEMBERING!

The Challenge of Spilyay — a challenge of survival — is told through three-dimensional dioramas, exhibits, pictures, buildings and sounds in the museum at the Yakima Nation Cultural Center, near Toppenish, which opened June 9, 1982.

The date for the opening was the 127th anniversary of the treaty which established the Yakima Indian Reservation and a new political entity. The Yakima Nation is composed of 14 separate but closely related tribes and bands.

The opening was a week-long celebration with runners carrying invitations to government officials across the mountains. Tony Washines, the last runner, presented his invitation to the mayor of Seattle.

Spilyay, that spirit of many shapes or no shapes at all, the trickster, the first great experiencer, teacher by example, is a very real legendary figure in Yakima Indian history. He often visited the Indians in the form of a coyote and taught them how to survive and live successfully with nature. These lessons are the basis of the museum's story, according to director Gary Young.

Among the many exhibits that depict life in the old days at the Yakima Nation Cultural Center Museum is this little girl with her basket ready to pick huckleberries.

The museum story was put together over a period of about two years basically by eight people — Agnes Tulee, Inez Strong, Hazel Umtuch, Don Umtuch, Delores Buck, James Selam, Jerry Lewis, Cynthia Mesplies and Jack Rebes — under the direction of Violet Rau. However, hundreds of people, young and old, participated through interviews, by collecting and preparing materials and by actual construction of one or more parts of this permanent exhibit.

Tulee, who now works in the administration office, says, "We didn't know where to start. But we had a lot of good help. Violet helped us, so did Helen Schuster and many others. We talked to the elders. We held many meetings and had lively discussions. Jack Rebes was the writer and Jerry Lewis the artist. We hired a professional, and were so proud when he said that we already had the story.

The museum exhibits take the observer from prehistoric times to the present — from the high country of the mountains to the lowlands of the Yakima Valley. The story tells the history, culture and heritage of the Yakimas by the Yakimas.

"Our heritage is so old that no one knows when it was born," say the elders. The exhibits start with a huge basalt rock signifying time before man and casts of ancient carvings thousands of years old. There's the legend of the eel and the sucker, who, as the story goes, bet each other their bones. Swimming side by side in the tank today, the eel has no bones and the sucker has more bones than any fish should have.

The museum provides a scenario of Celilo Falls, where the Indians gathered to harvest salmon, now covered by water backed up by The Dalles Dam. It is so real one almost feels as if he were there. Mose Thompson, who did the finishing work, lived in that area and remembers the falls as they were almost to each rock. Ted Palmateer painted the water, which looks as it were really flowing.

Center stage is the tule winter lodge where the extended family spent the cold months of the year. It was here that lessons were taught by the elders through legends. James Selam, who lived in one as a boy, collected and prepared the willows, poles, tules and hemp and supervised construction. Among his helpers were Elsie, Loretts and Loren "The Boy" Selam, Sarah Quaempts, Emma and John Telakish, Helen Jim, Amelia Sohappy, Diane Kanine Scott, Tony Warwick and Harrison Miller. The women spent days fashioning reed mats with hemp and rawhide used for sitting on, for sleeping on or a covering for the dead.

In the village there are also a tule tepee, an earth lodge built by John Moses, a storage pit for preserving food and a sweat house for cleansing the body and mind. A drop cloth painting of Mt. Adams (Pahto) overlooks the village as it has guarded the Indian land for eons.

The tule marsh has its own special significance to the Indian lifestyle. In the marsh is found the tule used in making the mats for housing and burial purposes. Here, too, the Indian people harvest hemp which is used for rope in building houses, making clothing and for fish nets such as Selam made for museum display. All tools and materials used in the making of the dip net were hand-made as they were before the coming of the white man. A hemp string calendar is used to count the days.

The first people to inhabit the land were proficient in the hunting and preservation of wild game, catching salmon and gathering wild plant foods. Gathering the food made a "people on the move" from spring migration to the traditional root grounds, the rivers and streams for the salmon runs, to the high country for huckleberries and game in the fall. Each season is related to their way of life, which was in rhythm with nature. To them earth and life were sacred. The land taught material and spiritual values. These seasonal efforts are part of the audiovisual dioramas.

Richard Cook, a muralist from San Francisco, played an important part in making the exhibits as realistic and effective as they are but he gives most of the credit to

All items in the Yakima Nation Cultural Center Museum are authentic. Those who made the various exhibits collected natural materials and built them by methods used in the old days as near as possible. Tule mats covered the winter lodge, sometimes several layers were used for warmth.

the tribe. "It's their story and their design in terms of the story line and its sequence," he emphasizes.

During the latter part of a tour of this unique museum that is both a story-telling and an artifact museum, one will see through pictures how life has changed for the Yakimas since the coming of the white man — housing, clothing, work, schools.

The museum is a vital part of the Yakima Nation Cultural Center. Completed and dedicated in 1980, the Center was nine years in the making. It is the result of years of hope, thought, planning and building on the part of the Yakima Tribal Council. It is the dream come true also of Nipo Strongheart, an honorary member of the tribe who was born near White Swan, became a movie star and well-respected lecturer, and who willed his vast collection to the Yakima Nation for its use and for all peoples of the Valley.

The dramatic complex of buildings is clustered about the 76-foot high winter lodge, available for conventions, banquets, trade shows and other events. The library serves as an educational facility for historical Indian research with several thousand books for the use of tribal members and residents of the area as well as some 10,000 volumes from the Strongheart collection available for research and inspection.

The theater presents first-run, family-type movies and performing arts. The Heritage Inn restaurant with Harris Teo, Jr., director, is open daily. The 14 Tribes Room is available for groups of up to 50. The winter lodge can seat 250. A gift shop offers hand-made articles. There is also a moccasin shop.

The museum is open daily 10 a.m. to 9 p.m., Sunday 10 a.m. to 6 p.m., with a small admission. Groups can be arranged with entertainment at times.

According to Young it is hoped the museum will preserve the traditions and culture of the Yakimas while at the same time serve as a communication between the Yakima Indians and other peoples of the valley.

Delores Buck, a Wanapum and one of the last of her people, helped with the construction of the Museum especially telling of the ways of the Old Ones.

Bob Moldanodo and his "Hawk Boy" plate. Others enjoying his work encourages him.

CERAMICS CENTER

Creativity is booming at the Yakima Indian Nation Ceramic Center as evidenced by dirty hands, dusty floor and smudged blue jeans.

On the perimeter of Toppenish, in the old garment factory, there may be a dozen or so people participating in this ancient art of ceramics. They find themselves as they work out their frustrations with the paint brush, the spray can or the feel of clay in their hands.

"It's a voluntary program. They may come and go as they please," says Mrs. May Dodd, director of the Yakima Indian Nation Comprehensive Alcoholism Program. "This is one project of our rehabilitation program."

Financed by a grant to begin with, it is becoming a healthy business as the lovely objects, (bowls, planters, plates, ash trays, etc.) are being discovered by area people. It is also appreciated by out-of-state visitors who desire a distinctive local product to carry home with them.

In the brightly lighted work room, Larry George, a well-known artist, author and educator, supervises the workers. Larry Freeman offers technical advice for mixing the clay, pouring it, cleaning the greenware painting and glazing. Unless it is a set of dishes, each piece is finished in an individual manner.

The designs on the ceramics are usually symbols of a natural phenomena. Examples of this are Bob Moldonado's "Hawk Boy" and George's "Elk." The Yakima Indians believe "My Mother is the Earth and My Father is the Light," and their cycle of living is linked to nature, the sacredness of earth as well as life on it. Their designs, therefore, to a great extent reflect their feelings.

Lightning is of particular significance to Moldonado (Ah-swan), who uses it in many of his works, relating it to the sun, moon and stars. On his "Hawk Boy," the feature bird is surrounded by lightning with the sun in the back, symbolizing the tie-in with the energy emitting from the bird.

Hours may be spent on design alone by this young Yakima Indian. His sketches are also popular at Indian fairs and shows. Once a design is done to his satisfaction it may be used in more than one project. Although he has always been interested in art, this is the first time Moldonado has given his time exclusively to the thing he likes best to do. "Others sharing in the enjoyment of my work encourages me," says Moldonado.

The elk, such as Larry George painted, supplied food for his ancestors, who revered the earth and took only game, fish, roots and berries to supply their needs.

If the individual does not want to make his own design, there are books to copy from, patterns and stencils to use. Colors of the designs are generally earthy; but blue sky and water are also predominant.

Usable pots of many sizes and shapes, platters, trays, cups, decorative pieces to set on the table or hang on the wall and sets of dishes (services of four or six; dishwasher safe), are ready for sale at the Center.

George and his crew are looking for outlets in the Pacific Northwest for their ceramic work, to make the program self-sustaining.

Perhaps this will be another recognition for the Yakima Indians, who have long been known as expert craftsmen of stone, buckskin and Klickitat baskets.

Creativity flourishes at the Ceramic Center.

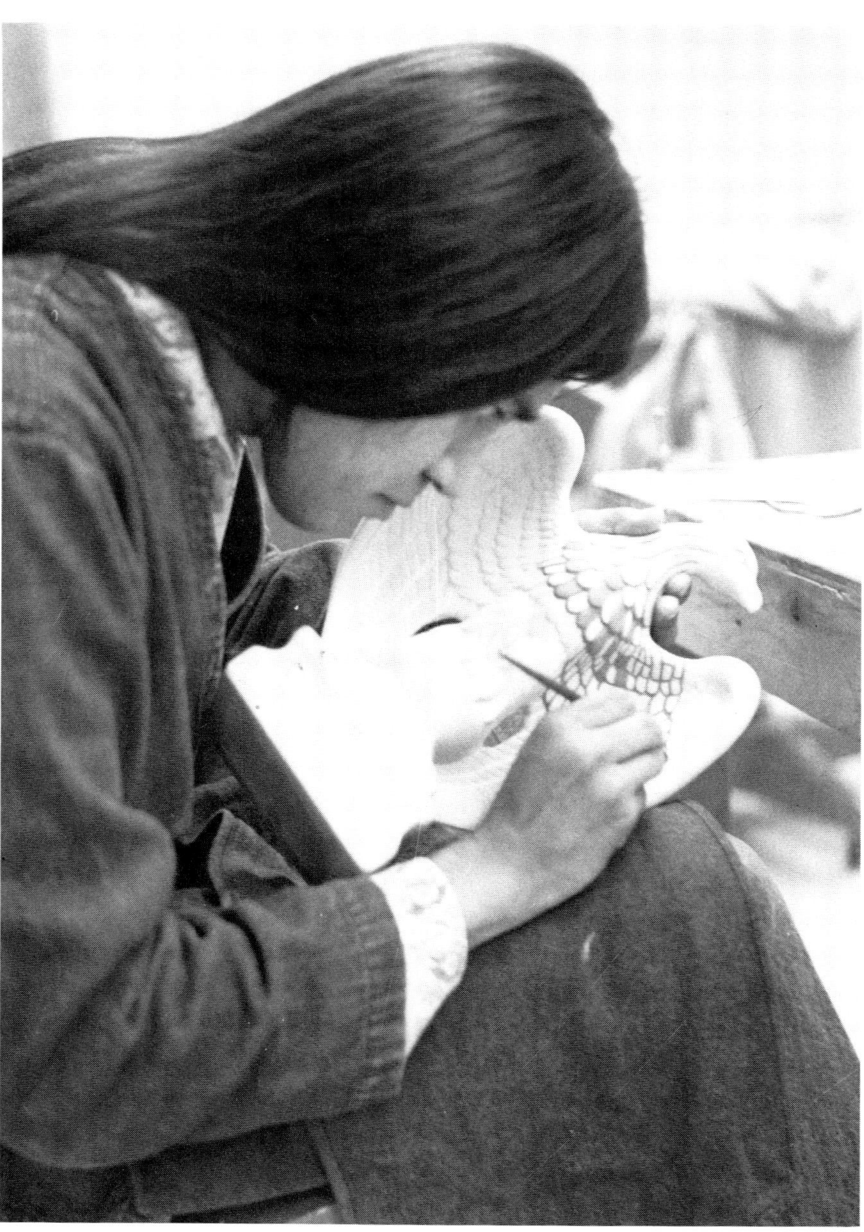

Workers at the Ceramic Center are intent on their subject. They work long hours to get "just that right effect".

Although Nettie and her husband, Alba Shawaway, had no children of their own, they helped to "raise" many. Though scattered far and wide Nettie still hears from them.

NETTIE SHAWAWAY

As Nettie Shawaway sits in her comfortable home with its shiny floors and big windows, sewing tiny glass beads on a canvas-type material, she reflects on some of the changes that have taken place in her lifetime.

Some of the changes have been good, she maintains, but some not so good. Nettie has accepted most of them, but still retains the gentle ways of people who live close to nature. She is of the Warm Springs tribe in Oregon, but when Nettie married Alba Shawaway, a Wanapum-Yakima, she came to live on the Yakima Reservation on land belonging to her late husband.

They spent many happy years together in a home that he admonished her not to leave even when he was gone. "He was a good man, a well-known and respected member of the Tribal Council, the governing body of the Yakima Nation." she says. He was also a cattle rancher, and friend and brother to Click Relander, author of *Drummers and Dreamers*, the only recorded history of the Wanapums.

As Nettie strings the beads on one thread, stitching them down crosswise with a second one every second bead, this active 76-year-old relates how their designs come from the heart or mind of the individual. They are geometric sometimes, or more intricate, using curved lines in florals, rodeo or human and animal figures. Colors are earthy, bright, or the blues of the sky and water. It is well known that the color combinations, design, balance and technical skill of the Plateau Indians' beadwork rival any of the so-called "fine arts." These are the Indians who live in eastern Washington, northern Oregon, inland British Columbia and Idaho. While the color and patterns have changed and grown in time, as have all things, the basic underlying spirit remains the same.

As an extension of cultural pride Nettie and Alba, (and later Nettie and her sisters), have taken their art forms to the World's Fair in Seattle, Expo at Spokane, the Smithsonian Institution in Washington, D.C. and other places to spark interest, awareness and compassion for native American handwork and a respect for creation by other people.

Nettie supports and participates in all activities of the Speelyi-mi Indian Arts and Crafts Club of which she and her husband were original members. She also attends and helps with many activities on the Yakima Reservation. In the spring she digs roots with the Wanapum women, who are "like the real Indians I grew up with. We sit on the floor for our feasts. We don't want to change this." It is here, too, that she practices the Washat religion.

She travels around the country in her "like new" pickup. There's a canopy over the back under which she carries a bed for warm weather use. Other times, she takes the mattress into the sleeping area of a home or building, depending on where she might be. When people come to the Speelyi-mi Fair or other events from far away places, Nettie beds them down in her own home in the same manner. The sprightly lady laughingly says, "last summer I drove my sister's van to the Crow dances in Montana. I love to dance." During the Pendleton Roundup, she and her sisters returned the hospitality by feeding two teepees of Crow who had come to participate in this well-known Pacific Northwest event.

As a child Nettie lived in an isolated area of their reservation, had little formal education, but learned the ways of her family and use of the natural resources. "We were poor, but healthy," comments the sparkly, dark-eyed widow. "My mother was a hard worker, but I learned to be self-sufficient and independent. We tanned the deer hides, scraping and soaking them for moccasins and clothes."

"One time my mother cut out many pairs of gloves. Each of us five girls had a part to sew. It was like an assembly line. We sold them to make money. We worked in the hops, too, going to the field on horseback or in wagons."

Nettie's hands are never idle. The designs she uses are ones from her heart...about the sun, moon, stars, earth, sky...

"We traveled to where the food was —to the river for salmon in the spring — what a pity we can't do that now. We took only what we needed for food." Steelhead, plentiful then, was needed for its oil or fat.

"In the fall we went to the hills for huckleberries. Then mother — who lived to be well over 100 years of age, would start the fire in a log to dry them. I can remember...sometimes the horses were purple from the juice. We also used service berries and choke cherries.

"Fall was deer hunting, too. There were no laws then about killing deer. We preserved the meat. Everything was good — the head, tongue and liver. The bones made the best broth for dumplings. The marrow was very good. We'de stay in the hills for about a month or until it was ready to storm."

"We raised a garden, dug roots — camas, onions and picked the sunflower plant when it was just coming out of the ground. It's like celery. We bought only rice, coffee and such. We boiled everything which, of course, is much healthier. Once in a while, we'd have fried potatoes. Carrots, potatoes, and turnips were stored in a pit in the ground, which was covered with straw. We raised chickens for meat and the eggs," she said, gesturing with her hands. "We lived in a one-room house with an attic, or in a wigwam sometimes."

Nettie learned to cook over a campfire. Later she cooked for many years in the government hospital on the Warm Springs Reservation.

Now and again, the lively little lady breaks out in some of the melodic expressions of her own people — or it may be the Yakimas or Wanapums. Sounds that seem to be drawn from nature — the song of the meadowlark or the falling rain.

This ambitious lady has considered moving to the Warm Springs reservation to be near her own people, but "I have so many friends here, Indians and whites. And it would be so hard to move my plants," she says as she points to the green ones reaching to the ceiling of her modest home.

Nettie had no children of her own, but she and her husband raised many "adopted" ones who remember her frequently, though they are scattered all over the country. While there's only one, herself, to feed she still cans and freezes whatever she can get "because I like to." She's generous with her preserved foods when it comes to celebrations, a trait she learned at home. It's a lonely life for one, but when there's so many things to do — beadwork, weaving, sewing her clothes, preparing and preserving foods, participating in ceremonials and tribal events. And so many people to care about, there's little time to think about oneself.

Nettie is a good story teller. She remembers the old days as well as more recent experiences.

As Nettie tells her stories, she may break into song — song of the birds, song of the wind or some other sound she hears in nature.

Kyonia Tecumseh and a friend who is ready for the dance contest.

KYONIA TECUMSEH

"I've danced in the White House for President and Mrs. Lyndon Johnson," says Kyonia Tecumseh as her black eyes sparkle. This vivacious black-haired Indian girl is the daughter of the late Chief Kiutus and his wife, Marie, a Winnebago. Kyonia lives on the Yakima Indian Reservation when she is not pursuing one of her many talents about the country.

While a student at the White Swan school she was "just an ordinary girl, an honor student, active in chorus, band, pep club and 4-H." Later, Kyonia transferred to the Institute of Indian Arts in Santa Fe, New Mexico. Here she studies traditional music and languages of the Southwest, the Northwest and Midwest Indians and of the Alaskans.

Then came the exciting opportunity to perform with the Indian Chanters and to help write the score for the performance at the White House. As guests of Secretary of the Interior Stuart Udall, the young performers had their first experience as movie stars.

This was not, however, Kyonia's first experience on the stage. The family accompanied her father, the well-known lyric tenor and lecturer about the country.

Kiutus was the great-grandson of the mighty chieftan, Tecumseh, who united the Indian nations against the whites. Kiutus' talents were discovered as he herded sheep in the mountains above the Yakima Valley. He was trained by Professor Dufresne at the Chicago Musical College. After he married, he brought his family into his act as he sang and talked of his people, their philosophy and conservation of the country's natural resources.

"Father was a naturalist, an environmentalist, a man ahead of the times," believes his daughter.

Kyonia is not sure when her first appearance on stage may have been. She has a picture from a Spokane newspaper showing her at six months of age on a baby board and captioned, "Baby Steals Show From Mighty Chief."

"You see, I'm a ham; always have been" she laughs.

"I'm like my father. He never knew a stranger. Neither do I." She talks with her hands and her shiny eyes as she brushed back a strand of hair.

"My father raised us so we would learn to be self-sufficient. We grew everything we ate. We would get wheat and corn from a nearby farmer and have the grain ground at the watermill at Union Gap. To this day, I can't stand cornmeal mush because I had to eat so much of it as a child."

"For several years my mother and father were leaders of the Real American 4-H Club. We learned to garden, to cook, to can, to sew, to raise animals and to exhibit at the fairs. We also learned parliamentary procedure and how to be leaders. We were encouraged, yes, pushed, into participating in all kinds of events and we were never to take a second. My father wanted perfection.

"We could have lived anywhere. My father had performed all over the country, including Carnegie Hall and the White House. But he wanted us to live in this beautiful picturesque Yakima Valley. We milked cows and churned our own butter. Also, father insisted that all of us have music lessons every Saturday.

"My father was broadminded. He wanted us exposed to all cultures of the valley and all religions; the Catholic, the Mormon, as well as the mysticism of our own people. I had business training at Haskell Institute in Lawrence, Kansas. My two brothers and two sisters have college degrees as do their spouses. But my father left his music to me. I am my father's child."

When hospitalized in Seattle, a whole new era opened up in her young life. Kyonia attended classes at the University of Washington, taught traditional Indian music and choreographed dances at the University Show Boat theater, represented the American Indian in the Seattle Model Cities Day-Care Program, and was queen of the Seattle Indian Center. Also, she taught sign language to deaf mutes at Goodwill Industries. "You see, one thing leads to another. It's so easy for me to learn and the rewards are so great working with these people."

Her father's admonition to "take whatever you have, use your hands and make something beautiful" was demonstrated when Kyonia was an occupational therapist working with Senior Citizens at a Yakima convalescent home. One of her attributes is patience — and the people responded because they loved her so. Every craft they entered at the Yakima Fair received a blue ribbon.

At one time, Kyonia was told by medical doctors that she might never walk again. But with her faith and prayers, and those of others, she was able to overcome her affliction. Like her father, Kyonia follows her heart. She knows she can do anything she puts her mind to.

This beautiful young lady with her scintillating manner has participated in beauty contests, clerked in a retail store, helped organize relief for flood victims, studied modeling and drafted programs for the teenager and the aged at the Spokane Indian Center.

Kyonia wonders where next her footsteps will take her. For one born in 1947, her life has been, as she says, "colorful and exciting, never dull." She's been torn at times with the clash of cultures and terribly frustrated, but..."I never see color. At one time I was eating with Orientals, studying black culture, serving as Miss Seattle Indian Center and living in a white world."

When things get tough she remembers "the gifts the Lord has given me. I've been told that my life is a mission. I must make it so. And undoubtedly something will happen soon to point the direction for me to go."

Kyonia has many talents and she uses them as she follows her heart into new places and things.

CONNIE AMBROSE

1972

She's 18.
She's beautiful.
Her eyes sparkle and shine.
Her smile is charming.
She walks with pride and grace.
She's Connie Ambrose, Miss Washington Universe.

Her perfect oval face with flawless olive complexion and long, dark hair were inherited from her father, a Yakima Indian.

Connie has lived in White Swan most of her life, but recently moved to Seattle for the last six months of her reign — where she will work in a department store (Nordstrom Best) and model for the Northwest Girl Agency — most of which she thinks will be in restaurant style shows.

While Connie is looking forward to this new experience — she takes everything as it comes — she is not as excited as some girls might be about living in the "big city".

She likes her home, her family, her neighbors and friends, and the open spaces of the Yakima Valley.

She loves to ride one of her horses — either the Cayuse Indian horse or a quarter horse — and feel the wind in her hair. She likes to bicycle and walk — even in the rain. Every walk is a nature trail to her as she finds tiny animals, plants and flowers bypassed by the unconcerned.

Wearing the crown of Miss Washington Universe is a responsibility — just as caring for her two sisters and three brothers, for over two years, was after the death of her mother, until her father remarried. But the latter was an experience she "wouldn't trade for anything." However, this work at home did not keep her from being an honor student or from participating in school and community activities. She was a member of the school drill team and Pep club, a song leader and she turned out for track. She worked on the school newspaper and journalism was a favorite subject.

Connie Ambrose, Miss Washington, 1972.

She is no stranger to "royal crowns". During her four years at White Swan high school where she graduated in 1972, she was a Christmas Ball princess and a Homecoming princess, a White Swan Rodeo junior princess and a princess in the Harrah Sugarbeet Festival.

She was also on the People's (a Yakima department store) high school fashion board — and this is where the Miss Washington Universe all began.

Connie remembers the excitement of flying first class with the girls from the Pacific Northwest to the Miss U.S.A. contest in New York City, the friendly people of Puerto Rico, the $1,500 evening gown she wore, the rehearsals, the thrill of seeing her father, grandmother, two brothers and her former employers. Mr. and Mrs. Pete Mullinex, at the contest — but most of all she values the friendships made during this event-filled fourteen days, May 7-22, 1972. She corresponds frequently with girls from Montana, California, Kansas and Arizona.

While she did not place in the contest —(she was the youngest contestant) she says, "I met many nice people. There were many rewards. All the people I met will help me form my life".

Each event in which she has participated in Eastern Washington — the Lilac Festival in Spokane; as Grand Marshal in the Sunnyside parade; as judge of the Miss Sunnyside pageant; openings at the Yakima Valley Mall; Sunfair at the Central Washington fair, Yakima; and grand opening of Mohler barber school, Yakima, under the new ownership of the regional director of the Miss Washington Universe contest and her chaperone. Mr. and Mrs. Harold Larson — has been graced with her charm and at the same time has helped to shape her life.

After this year, which she is enjoying to the fullest as she represents us all, what then? She hasn't decided, but three options seem to appear at the present time as most interesting: an airline stewardess, a legal secretary, or living in Europe with a family where she could learn the culture of a particular country.

As a legal secretary she might work with her brother, who is graduating this year from White Swan High and who intends to become a lawyer; specifically, an Indian lawyer. In this way, she could help develop and maintain the Indian culture.

She says she really has no big plans for a career. She feels the most important thing is to be a good wife and mother. For this she has a background in sewing, cooking, woodworking, ceramics and yardwork. She likes doing every one of them, especially while listening to music which may be anything from hard rock to Beethoven.

Her father, a forest technician and her younger brothers and sisters will miss Connie, but it is almost a sure thing that she will return to "her valley".

With her abilities and her charm, poise, beauty and personality, she may be sidetracked for a while — but no matter what Connie does she will like doing it. She is that kind of person.

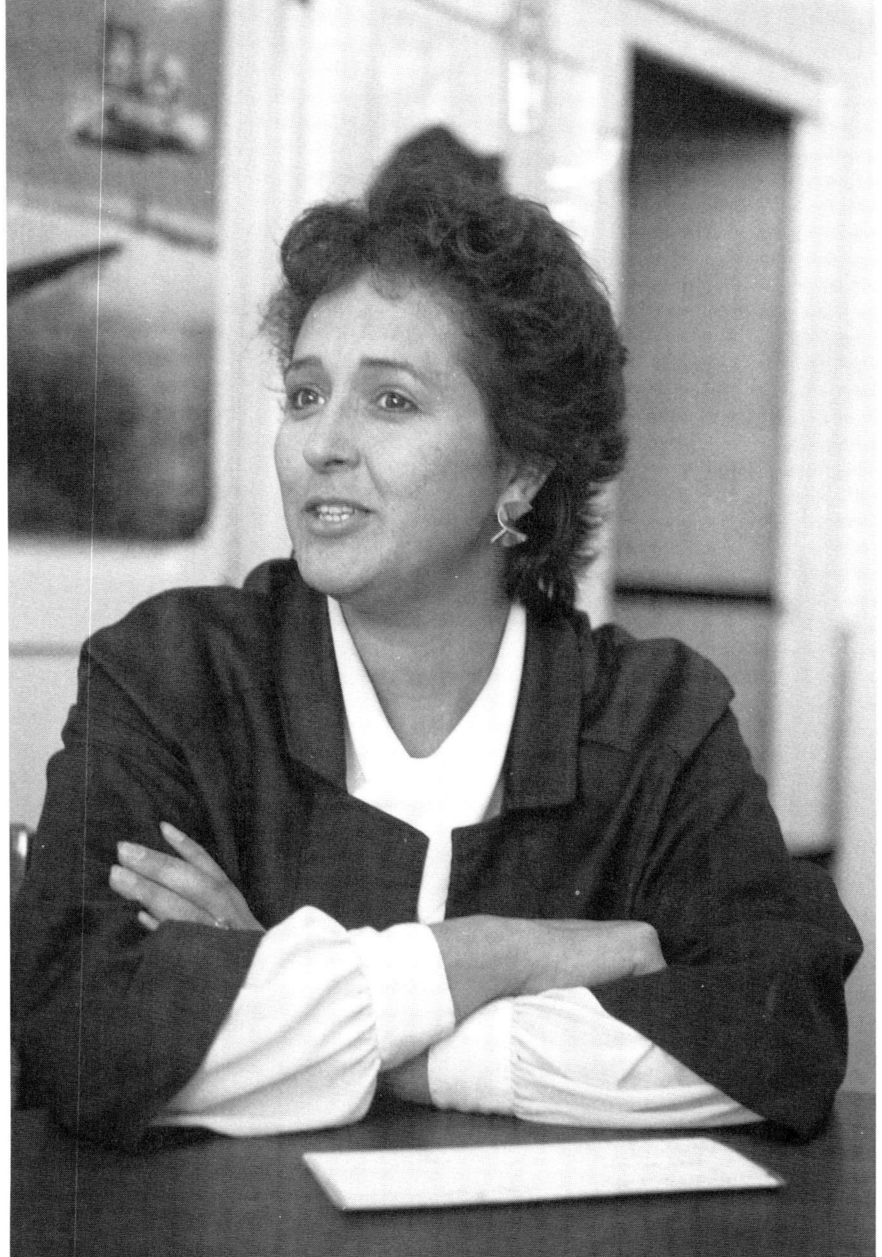

Connie Ambrose, 1988.

THE DOOR OPENED

When Connie Ambrose was Miss Washington Universe she said, "All the people I meet in my experiences will help form my life." Today she says, "How true! How true!"

Her experiences have trained her well for her position as director of the academic skills center and assistant professor at Heritage College, Toppenish.

This enrolled Yakima was an honor student at White Swan High School, where she remembers having been princess at several school events, and also her English teacher, Bess Clyde, who cautioned her, "Don't close the doors on opportunity." "Her influence had a great impact on where I am today," said Connie.

Connie realized that wearing the crown of Miss Washington Universe was a responsibility — as was caring for her two sisters and three brothers two years after her mother died, until her father remarried.

"Modeling in Seattle helped me with poise and contacts, but no one told me when I entered Shoreline Community College that I couldn't or shouldn't sign up for 27 hours credit." She passed two courses and dropped the rest. Classes in chemistry changed her mind about being a nurse.

While a student at Smartlowit Center, Bertha Ortega noted her bewildered look and encouraged her to enroll at Eastern Washington State University. She did, and received a BA in speech communication and a teaching certificate.

Several years were spent at Stanford, where her husband was on the faculty and she was a student part-time. She enjoyed living in the international environment where their home was located. She received her MA in administration and policy analysis from Stanford.

Connie directed the Indian teacher education program at Humboldt State University, Eureka, California before coming to Heritage College in 1985, "in her valley." She is also involved in several national programs, for which she travels to Washington, DC on occasion.

Heritage College, with 311 students, had its first graduation in May 1986. It offers education to a multicultural rural population of the Yakima Valley. Average age of the students is 29. Many of the students are returning to school after a long absence, and are in need of more advice on their class schedule.

The soft-spoken, articulate 33-year-old advises students who are searching for their niche. She assists them in selecting appropriate classes. Among the students are a number of single parents who are working part- or full-time. Being a single parent herself, with three children aged two, three and five, she can relate to these students. She admonishes them, "Don't close the doors. Take time to develop your emotional and spiritual side as well as your health.

"I enjoy teaching. It brings out the animated side of me. When you're doing what you like to do, it shows." Her classes include computer science.

Connie grew up at a time when Indians were being "assimilated." "Because my grandparents were punished at school for being Indians, my parents did not want us to be so affected. Having a Yakima for a father and a non-Indian for a mother, I could go either way. Now that we are going back to the old ways, I'm trying to learn and teach my children about Indian culture.

"During the summer we built a sweathouse and used it. We went to the mountains for huckleberries and to the hills for roots. I am taking my children to the Indian church. We are learning respect for the land and for the water. I want my children to understand that they can do anything as adults. There are so many opportunities for both men and women today.

"I hope that I can relate our Indian culture to the students with whom I am associated. This year at Heritage there is 51% Caucasian, 21% native American, 24% Hispanics, 4% Negro or Asian and 8 international students," she commented.

Connie sees more opportunities in the future. She wants to complete her studies for a doctorate degree, she'd like to work in the Washington, DC area and perhaps in some third-world country. But she will return to her valley when she retires.

Connie's Indian name, Latite (Flower), given to her by her grandfather, was well chosen. She has blossomed, and is able to help others do likewise.

SHOWCASE OF HERITAGE

When you step into the Twin Red Barn Museum on Highway 97 south of Toppenish, a mannequin wearing a dark turquoise dress of Hudson's Bay trade cloth and lavishly decorated with beads will catch your eye. She wears moccasins, a turquoise necklace, carries a rawhide bag in one hand and in the other three eagle feathers . You may be amazed to learn that this dress, once the property of a prominent Yakima Indian family, is more than 200 years old. It is in good condition, but a recent owner added bright red ribbon and a gold braid on the hem and sleeves with a sewing machine!

Standing next to this mannequin is another wearing a wedding dress, complete with veil. The dress is also of Hudson's Bay trade cloth and its decoration is a yoke of dentalium shells. The shredded ribbon on the hem reveals that this dress is also old —150 years or more. The veil, or cap, is also of dentalium shells, and the mannequin wears Chinese coins in her hair!

In contrast is a "modern," 75-year-old buckskin dress trimmed with weasel fur, beaded belt and shell necklace.

Bud Swindler holds two dancing sticks from the collection of Indian artifacts at the Red Barn Museum near Toppenish.

If antique Indian dresses don't interest you, perhaps the feather headdresses will — or shelves of baskets, the collection of buckskin bags, the dancing sticks, or the bustles work by the men in contest dancing made of brightly colored feathers. There's petroglyphs salvaged from the Columbia Gorge before the water from the dams covered so many priceless Indian artifacts. There's a pair of silver spurs, paintings and drawings by local artists, including a huge one of Eagle Salatsee, bowls and pestles from the early days and picture frames full of arrowheads.

Glassware and other relics of the pioneers, and even items from our fathers' and grandfathers' day, line the shelves and showcases.

Owners of this small, interesting museum— and rock shop — are Gloria Stanton, a Yakima who grew up on the reservation, and Bud Swindler, who came from a Wyoming reservation. She is a collector, and saved everything. He hunted arrowheads and other Indian artifacts as a youngster, but sold what he found.

Bud is also a rockhound, a professional who dug rocks of many kinds from all over the northwest to supply rock shops with whatever they needed. He is also a trader.

Gloria Stanton holds two Levi dolls. These dolls, dressed in Levis and Indian blankets were an advertising gimmick in the 1920's.

He started the Twin Red Barn Rock Shop about four years ago. When their house began to bulge about three years ago and they found they had many interesting items to share with others, they started the small museum also. Bud's ability to buy, sell and trade has brought many additional articles, and now the museum is full.

When you stop at the Twin Red Barn Rock Shop and Museum, be sure you have some time. The friendly owners will explain the use of the artifacts, and perhaps how they acquired them. Gloria will show you the Levi's dolls — Indian dolls wearing Levi's under their blankets, an advertising item from the 1920's. She may also show you her collection of earrings, those she has worn during her lifetime.

Bud will show you the dancing sticks, the silver spurs, feather headdresses and then perhaps take you to the rock shop, where he has amethysts, garnets, thunder eggs, petrified wood and other rocks, as raw material or ready for jewelry. He may show the beautiful Ellensburg blue agates that he is finishing, how he slices the hard material with diamond-edged saws or polishes garnets.

Don't fail to notice the wristband Gloria wears, or the barrette — made by a daughter — in her long dark hair. Gloria has passed on some of her handicraft talents, almost a lost art among today's Indians.

A local silversmith, local artists and local seamstresses provide articles for the museum and for sale in the shop — ribbon shirts or blouses, earrings, many kinds of jewelry, paintings and drawings. They can also repair beadwork and such.

The Spokane to Portland summer bus stops for a few minutes when there is time for a quick look into the museum and rock shop to buy, sell or trade.

Visitors have registered from all over the world. One of the more recent was a native from Africa, who had come to this country to study the reservation system.

Gloria and Bud will tell you some intriguing stories about their experiences. They might even tell about mining in Idaho... but that's a story in itself.

The Rock Creek Longhouse where Pow-wows and other celebrations are held, attracting dancers and drummers and those who just like to go to Pow-wows from a large area.

Guests come from Pendleton, Warm Springs, and sometimes from Seattle, for the annual Mother's Day dinner at Toppenish. A number of the elderly ones are selected for special honors. If any food is left over it is put into cartons or plastic bags and sent home with the guests, a tradition of the past when tribes and bands met for pow-wows and sharing of their bounty.

Lucy John practices some of the "old ways." She weaves baskets, bags, designs and makes decorated buckskin gloves, vests and moccasins for herself, for friends or to sell. She collects and preserves (dries) roots and other wild plants for food.

Lucy John and her husband, Simon, lived in this house some eight miles up Satus Creek for 13-14 years. The house was moved to an acreage along the Granger cutoff, between Highways 12 and 97 where it stands today...in back of her modern, all-electric home. It will stand there the rest of her days.

NEW HOMES

Before the snow flies, Lucy John will move into a new, all-electric home. So will Theodore Phillips, Ronald McFee, Larry George, James Telakish, Tony Phillips and some 60 other Yakima Indian families.

At a meeting called at the Long House nearly eight years ago, the possibility of homes for low-income families built under a mutual aid program was discussed. Land was available for landless families, through a tribal "set-aside" of the early 1930's.

Lucy John and her husband Simon, were among the first to apply for a home and offer to do their share of the building; 400 hours for a three bedroom house, 450 hours for a four bedroom house.

Now a widow, with only one of her children at home, (and he only during the summer,) Lucy will enjoy the comfort of a well-built, warm, easy to care for home for the rest of her days.

Simon built their first home with about $200 worth of lumber. It was isolated, some eight miles up Satus Creek. After the older children went off to college, the house was moved to a piece of property they bought along the Granger cutoff between Highway 12 and Highway 97. Here they saw the rest of their youngsters graduate from Granger High School and start off for further education. All have graduated from college except the younger who is still attending CWSC.

Lucy John moved into her comfortable new all-electric home in 1972. That was the year some 80 homes were built for members of the Yakima Indian Nation.

The house, with some additions, which was their home for 13-14 years, still stands, minus one of the added-on rooms which is used for storage. It will remain, Lucy says, as long as she lives, just in back of her new home.

Larry George, well-known Indian artist and Lucy's son will live next door with his wife Tucelia and their young family. The home stands on an acre of land, deeded to him by his mother. This is the usual amount preferred for single dwellings.

While the home will be completely modern with thermostatically controlled base-board heating, no-wax vinyl floor covering and fiberglass all-in-one piece bath and shower, the decor will be totally Indian; not just Northwest Indian but All American Indian. As they have waited for their new home, the Georges' have collected plaques from the coast, Crumble prints from the Sioux, a Navaho clock, Sioux pottery, silk screens from the Lummi. Nathan Olney, another Yakima Indian artist, is designing the material for their curtains and drapes. George says they have a couple of Charles Russell paintings that they like, and he will do some of his own, along with some carvings to complete the decorations.

Each new home owner must work 400 or more hours on his or another home.

A few applicants have dropped out of this "Turnkey Mutual Aid Program." The responsibility was too great for them perhaps, but for others it has been an incentive to work or to better their jobs.

Martin Schwartzenberger is in charge of this HUD (Housing Urban Development) program. He tells us the homes are scattered about the Valley; 10 in the White Swan area, 15 at Goldendale, others are in clusters of two to four or single.

A developer builds the units, sells them to the Housing Authority, who approves them and pays for them with HUD funds. Repayment is according to ability which will be reviewed and adjusted annually.

The 1300 square feet three bedroom and the 1700 square feet four bedroom houses were designed by a local architect for convenience, permanency and ease in maintenence.

A committee of five, all Indians, selects the applicants deemed most worthy according to need, income and available land.

Ray Hoptowit, foreman under the Indian Housing Authority, inspects the houses as they are being built, checks for work the home-owner to-be can do and assigns such. The work need not be on his own home.

For those who need help and direction in caring for these new, modern homes in the $20,000 value range, the County Extension Service has cooperated with a Home Owners Short Course. In it are included operation of equipment — thermostats, pumps, fans, appliances — money management, landscaping, home care, and for those who desire, sewing primarily draperies and curtains.

Before the houses were started, each applicant selected the siding, roofing and room colors from several choices available. When the houses are turned over to the owners, they will be complete, ready for their own appliances and furniture. Although all are from the same basic design, each will be individual.

For Lucy, who has been living in an apartment in Wapato and for those who waited patiently through miles of red tape, in administration, hours of work, disappointments, changes and delays, their dreams will soon come true, and one of the big problems for the Yakimas, housing, will be partially solved.

AUNTIE GRACE

At White Swan Middle School there's a lady known as "Grandma Gracie" or "Auntie Grace." Her title is "home visitor," but she actually does anything that needs to be done — bandaging a sore finger, taking a sick child home, encouraging a student to do better school work, chaperoning a field trip, or barbecuing salmon or elk for the annual high school banquet.

She admits she likes to talk, but she has a "listening ear and the broad shoulders that go with it." She's the confidante of the little tykes at Harrah School; maturing girls and football heroes; teachers and parents; her own Indian people, in addition to whites and Mexican-Americans.

Mrs. Grace Ambrose has no formal education for this position — just years of experience. She has held the position the past three years and may have to give it up when she turns seventy next March.

Grace was born on the reservation out toward Fort Simcoe. She recalls roaming the hills; attending crawdad feeds; and swimming in Toppenish Creek.

After her parents separated, she and her brothers and sisters were on their own most of the time.

Her schooling at White Swan, Fort Simcoe and Chemawa, an Indian boarding school near Salem, Oregon, lasted only through the seventh grade. This may be why she repeats emphatically to her own family, to relatives, to foster children and others, "No matter what else you do, get an education. Girls as well as boys. Should it become necessary, you can get a good job and earn a living."

In 1927, Grace and Phillip Ambrose werre married, and she went to the hills with her sheepherder husband. Even after the children arrived much time was spent in summer sheep and cattle camps. The family has always done things together. When the girls wanted to be Campfire Girls, mother Grace became a leader as there was no group out where they lived. Later it was 4-H. She hauled kids and horses for the riding club and was instrumental in getting cooperation of the Bureau of Indian Affairs and the Yakima County Extension Service in setting up a loan whereby the youngsters could purchase animals to raise and show, and repay with dollars or progeny.

Traveling with and transporting youngsters to school and sports events, to club affairs, war dance contests, in addition to following her own son during his participation in sports, was time-consuming but enjoyable for one who likes people so well.

The Ambrose home has always been a gathering place. As the children grew up and brought their friends home, Grace never knew how many were going to show up for weekend breakfasts. A niece came to live with them, then other relatives and eventually foster children with whom the Ambroses shared their bounty and their love. There was always plenty because Grace believed in "waste not, want not." Elk and berries from the hills, salmon from the river, produce from their garden provided food. What was not eaten fresh, was preserved — hundreds of cans of vegetables and jars of fruit. Even today there's great fun when the family — children and grandchildren — get together to shuck and can corn at the custom cannery.

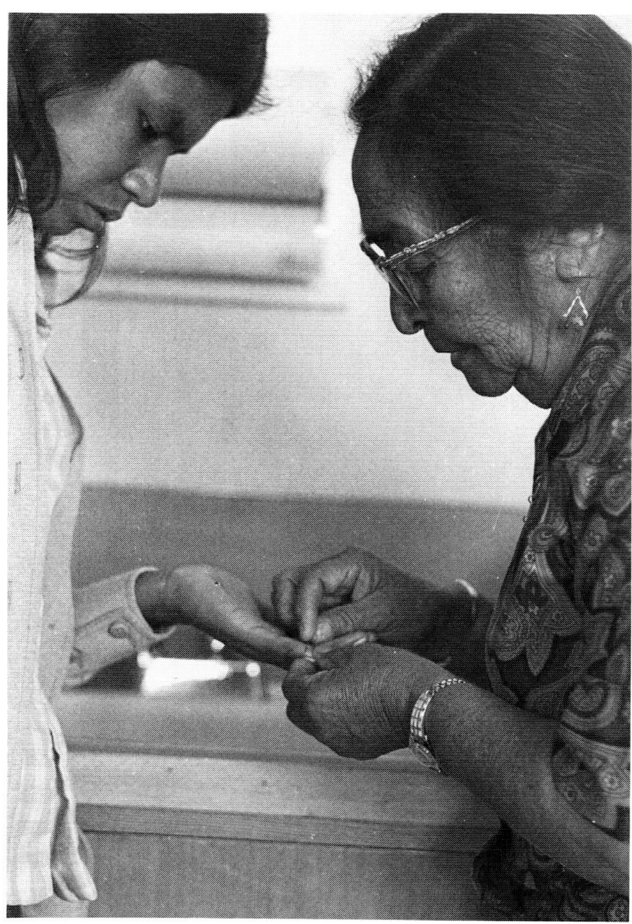

The extended family and friends come out to help with the cattle drives to and from the summer mountain pasture. Sharing, such a natural part of Gracie's life, has "rubbed off" on the grandchildren. During "Show and Tell" time at school, they shared some of Grandma Gracie's stories. Then Grandma Grace would come to school and tell more stories, first to one class and then another, until it became a day or two each week. Encouraged by her family she finally signed on officially because, "if she could help one child she would be doing some good!" She's commended by the teachers, principals and parents because she is someone who cares; someone who has the time to listen or talk to the students, teachers and parents. All this has resulted in a lower drop-out rate at the White Swan School.

In the community, this vivacious lady with sparkling, dark eyes and boundless energy is known for her elk stew, Indian fried bread, huckleberry pie and jam, as well as baked salmon. These may be sampled at the All-Indian Rodeo held in early June of each year, or at a number of other events, generally sponsored by the Reservation Improvement Club. This organization provides educational funds to help Indian children married outside the reservation and who are not eligible for tribal help, and for other families in need. She's a member of the Wigwam Club, a service club; is active in St. Mary's Catholic Church; attends educational meetings of the Johnson O'Malley Consortium; and helps wherever she may be needed.

This grandmother still rides a horse, does bead work, makes baby boards, sews, and takes her grandsons fishing after she cures salmon eggs for bait.

To keep in shape, she practices with the "Little Beavers," a peewee basketball team which she manages, coaches and transports from school to the Job Corps gym. She sees that the boys do stamina-strengthening exercises and instills sportsmanship as they play. Last year the Little Beavers were league and tournament champions.

Homemaker of the Year was an honor bestowed upon Grace in the late 1950's. More important to her, she has seen her own three children and many foster ones graduate from high shcool and pursue further education. Phillip, Jr., is a forestry technician and school board member. Theresa (Mrs. Joe) Sampson is a social worker, and Lila Whalawitsa is associate tribal judge and is a tribal social representative for HEW. A granddaughter, Connie Ambrose, reigned as Miss Yakima and later as Miss Washington Universe.

In September of this year, Grace was among 62 Yakimas who went to Washington, D.C. for the 10th annual festival of American Folklife sponsored by the Smithsonian Institution. She laughingly comments, "I worked my way through Washington, D.C.," as she was so busy setting up and explaining displays of Indian baskets, bags and roots, and preparing stew and Indian bread that she hardly had time to see the sights of the capital city. She was also a counselor, took care of the little ones and young people and administered to the needs of all. Fortunately, the root medicine which she had prepared and taken with her was not needed.

Grace respects Indian culture and traditions. While she preserves and promotes the past, she remains actively a part of the present. Grace declares she and her family are among the wealthiest people on earth, because "those who have friends are wealthy."

How do Gracie's family and friends feel about her?

They answer with one word. "She's beautiful."

Dorothy Sturm has an important job, and she performs it with characteristic warmth and competence.

LOOK OUT

Dorothea Sturm has the whole world in her hands — or as much of it as she can see from the top of Satus Peak.

She is the only lookout on duty on the vast Yakima Indian Reservation from early spring until late fall, and from her perch 4,180 feet above the valley floor, Dot can keep an eye on all corners of the 1,200,000-acre reservation and far beyond. To the north she can see across the valley to Ahtanum Ridge, to the east as far as the Rattlesnake Hills and Snipe's Mountain, and the tip of snow-capped Mt. Hood is visible to the south. As she completes the 360-degree turn — something she has done many times — she finds majestic Mt. Adams dominating the western horizon.

Dot can enjoy the legend of Goat Rocks as she picks out the mouth, nose, eyebrows, feathers, neck, chest, stomach and feet of the old Indian chief said to be resting there between courting visits to Mt. Hood, Mt. Adams and Mt. Rainier. On clear days she can even see Mt. Rainier and the Stuart Range northwest of Ellensburg.

Being a "fire-watcher" has been an experience from the very beginning. When Dot reported for work the first day she was asked to drive a jeep, a vehicle in which she had never ridden before. After a few quick instructions she and her boss were on their way. Dot was behind the wheel, following a fast-traveling lead car. Just beyond Satus Pass they turned off onto a narrow, winding road for five miles to Sopelia Lookout. "My boss pointed out a few peaks and valleys for identification points and told me that after four or five years I'd know the country," Dot recalls. "He didn't know that I was only planning to work one year." He apparently knew something Dot didn't know, because that exchange occurred 17 years ago!

After several years at Sopelia Lookout Dot was moved to her present location near the center of the reservation, where there is also a TV microwave relay and the radio relay for the Yakima Nation. Even though it is less remote, Dot may be on duty for a full ten-day shift without seeing another human being. She uses the radio to stay in constant contact with people. "The radio is turned on when I arrive in the spring," she says, "and is never off until I leave in the fall."

There have been fires, lightning, rattlesnakes and high winds, but anecdotes about the wind tend to dominate Dot's conversation. Her new steel-and-cement structure was necessitated by the unusual wind conditions. Winter winds have been estimated as high as 150 miles per hour.

"You can't understand how the wind blows up here unless you have experienced it," she laughingly comments. "When Western Tele-Communications set up their microwave it was rigged to stand 125-mile-an-hour winds, but it blew down the first winter. We even lost part of the roof off this new building the first winter it was here.

"When the wind gets too bad I take my sleeping bag, radio, book and light and move to the cement communications building which is a few steps away. I've had to crawl to it when the wind would knock me down, and one time I thought I was going over the cliff!

"Another night when I was still in the old wood building the windows on the southwest side of the lookout started breaking and the glass was blown all over — even onto my bed, which was in the far corner, I got up but didn't turn on the light. I really didn't want to see what was happening. I tried to call my boss on the radio at his home but he couldn't understand me. He recognized my voice and knew that I was in trouble. Finally the Glenwood Ranger Station came on and talked to my boss.

Immediately the air cleared and we could converse easily. As soon as they could make it, the men came for me — but I thought the wind would blow the pickup over as we went down the mountain.

"Have you ever seen lightning strike the ground?" she asks. "Sometimes it drills right into the ground, other times it hits with a pop. One time a ball of fire hit the ground right across the road from where I was standing. I tingled all over and got a headache from it, and I know my hair stood on end. You don't talk on the radio when there's a storm. Believe me, you learn to respect nature when you're up here."

Dot has seen her share of fires — grass fires, timber fires, brush fires. The worst ones are caused by lightning, but she has seen people start them, too.

"Everything stops when a fire is reported. If it's a grass fire the firemen come from the warehouse at Toppenish. If it's a timber fire the Signal Peak crew answers. The thinners and markers in the forest drop their tools and come to help, too."

Dot is always alert to car lights in the valley. She can see them from Sunnyside to Ft. Simcoe. She's especially concerned if they are in the canyon below because there is no reason for anyone to be there at night. One night she watched a car just below her, and after it left there was a puff of smoke and then flames. With her binoculars in one hand and the microphone in the other she reported to headquarters. Messages were relayed to Law and Order, and as she kept reporting the police were able to intercept the car near White Swan.

As Dot scans the horizon and checks the dust devils in the lower valley she tells of another unforgettable experience. "I went outside for something and thought the door was propped open, but when I came back it was locked. I pushed and shoved to no avail, so I started to walk out for help. But I hadn't gone far when I realized that all six keys for the lookout were in the drawer of the desk inside. I went back, stopped and asked the Lord for help. I gave one more big push, the door opened, and I fell flat on my face. I just lay there and said over and over, "Thank you, Lord, thank you." She immediately went outside again and hid a key under a rock. Now she wears one on a chain around her neck.

Benton REA supplies power to the lookout, which has all of the conveniences of a modern home — electric range, refrigerator, freezer, heaters, good lighting, hot and cold running water, formica-covered cabinets and a vacuum cleaner to keep up with the carpeted floor. There's even a television set, although it is seldom used. Whatever time Dot doesn't spend staring out the windows is used for reading — "I love to read," she says.

Considering what Dot can see from her windows, it's no wonder the television rates a poor third.

Sunrises and sunsets can be breathtaking, and the many varieties of wild flowers in the spring are something to behold. "I can pick out eight varieties in one spot," she says.

And there is always activity, even in the open country above the tree line. Wild horses, birds, sage rats, ground squirrels, chippies and pack rats can all be counted on for regular performances.

Perhaps Dorothea doesn't actually have the whole world in her hands, but she keeps her careful eyes on a big chunk of it.

On a clear day Dorothea Sturm can see forever or so it seems....all over the Yakima Indian Reservation to snow capped peaks, Mt. Adams, Mt. Hood and Mt. Rainier. Occasionally she has visitors.

MEDICINE VALLEY SCHOOL

The Medicine Valley School may not look exactly like it did when it was built, or even in 1937 when it was abandoned, but it's as nearly like the original as possible with today's materials.

Restoration of this landmark — an eyesore for years — came about at a family reunion of the Arquette family, who live nearby. Leonard Arquette made a chance remark to his aunt, Geneva Becker, "Why don't you buy that old school and move up here?"

Mrs. Becker had lived in the area off and on. Some of her fifteen brothers and sisters had learned their ABC's in this school. For over twenty-five years the children from this end of the valley started their education in the old white schoolhouse. In 1937, the dirt road to White Swan was graded, and the younger children boarded buses along with their brothers and sisters. The old schoolhouse was abandoned.

When Mrs. Becker was married, she and her husband settled in the Portland, Oregon area and developed a small family farm in the Tualatin Valley. Together they built their own home, barn, corrals and outbuildings, even though employed full time elsewhere. When her husband died she moved into a home in Portland, That was her situation when she attended the family reunion and heard Leonard's chance suggestion.

Mrs. Becker thought about the school. Although dilapidated, it had a good foundation, a necessary item if a building was worth renovating. She looked beyond the broken windows and faded siding and envisioned the old building bright with paint surrounded by a trim and neat yard with shaded trees.

To one who had shot deer for the family larder, bears, too, shingled roof and worked as a waitress, the task of restoring the old school did not seem formidable. Geneva remembered her grandmother, aged 90, ceiling in the back porch, "because she lived away out where there was no help." And Mrs. Becker's mother too, could do carpentry and "most anything."

When she approached her son about her plans he replied, "It's an awful mess. The easiest way would be to set a match to it. But... if you want to, we can do it!" Before the school was turned into the modern, all-electric home it now is, her family, relatives and friends became involved in tearing out, replacing, plumbing, painting, gardening, and a myriad of other details.

It took about a year to purchase the property. On the Yakima Reservation, the federal government held the property in trust for the Yakima Indians until the County obtained it for a school. Mrs. Becker, a tribal member, had the land returned to trust status.

Mrs. Becker set her camper on the school grounds, which was to be her home for six months. Remodeling began on June 13, 1972. Her sons, Charles and Frank, assisted her on their days off and weekends. Geneva did the cooking in a "cook shack" as she called it — a screened garden house — until severe summer windstorms blew the structure down.

When she purchased the place she was told there was always plenty of water, but after installing a new pump the well soon went dry. All that first summer they carried water from her nephew Leonard Arquette's place, and went to his nearby home for baths.

By the time the cook shack was demolished, it was getting to be cold weather; so she moved into the unfinished school on December 13, 1972. The building was warm with extra insulation in the ceilings and walls. At Christmas, an electric hot plate was a welcome gift to add to the electric skillet and toaster she'd been using. The dining table was a piece of plywood set on a tool box and the seats were boards covered with brightly covered oil cloth placed on grease cans turned upside down. Her kitchen cupboards were two sawhorses with planks laid across.

If Mrs. Becker had not wanted to restore the school to its original appearance, the remodeling would have gone faster. But she wanted it to look the way the old residents remembered it.

After much searching, shiplap identical to the original was discovered in a Yakima store. Over this, the original builder had installed four-inch cedar siding. This was impossible to find, but aluminum siding in the same size was available and one has to look carefully to realize it is aluminum rather than wood.

The original "two-by-sixes" were in good shape, preserved by the dry climate. But the old wood shingles had been covered with composition ones. The remodelers removed them all, laid new building paper and shingled the roof with new cedar shingles identical to the originals.

The only change in appearance came about when Mrs. Becker had the 12-foot ceiling lowered and new aluminum window frames installed. The high window line of the school is broken by a horizontal line marking the new ceiling height.

The house is a spacious 26 by 43 feet, all on one floor, with two bedrooms and two baths. A basement has been dug beneath the building to provide storage. One of the school closets was just the right size for a bath near one of the bedrooms. The room with the two-inch thick boards, where wood was stored and where naughty children were sent, (according to a sister who attended the Medicine Valley School), is now a utility room, with cabinets carved by son Frank.

Elegant kitchen cabinets in warm wood tones fit into the old-fashioned aura of the building. Custom built furniture, designed and made by Ronald Cheney, a friend, from oak barrels upholstered with bright vinyl add to the rustic but modern decor. Barrels have been used for lamp bases. Ceramic barrels hold flour, sugar and condiments.

Mrs. Becker located a pot-bellied stove to be set in the same location as the one when school was held there. It will be set up and connected to the original chimney when time permits. "It might come in handy some day," she commented. "But Benton Rural Electric is real dependable even in this remote place."

There's green grass around the white building; colorful petunias, wild yellow roses, nasturtiums, cosmos, marigolds. and zinnias; and a flag flutters in the breeze. The huge garden put in this year by her son and daughter-in-law, who are building nearby but living temporarily with Mrs. Becker, provides food for the table now and for winter preserving. Fruit trees, (apple, apricot, cherry and peach), supply fresh fruit at intervals during the summer, as do strawberries and raspberries. There's even herbs for flavoring. "About all we buy in the winter is milk, sugar, flour and coffee. I've even learned to bake my own bread."

It was a big project to find a bell similar to the one which called the little tykes to class at Medicine Valley School, but a bigger effort was to dig up and move cement blocks for both the bell and the flag pole when Geneva wanted them in a better location.

"It was fun, every bit of it," muses Mrs. Becker. "Every day, that is, except one... the day that I wanted to cry. It was hot and I was up high on a ladder trying to patch a board that had split. I said to my son, "Let's quit and go to Oregon, and get cooled off." We went to Portland. But would you believe it was a degree hotter there? We stayed all night, came back the next day refreshed and ready to tackle our job again.

Since last spring a heart stress has curtailed her activities and she's growing impatient. She wants to finish the entry way using some of the pupil's desks, sort out and display some of her several barrels of rocks collected in her travels about the country, finish her "spool" picnic table, find two more rake seats for the picnic table, plant more flowers. And also...

She's bought an old building in White Swan. It has a "good foundation," but needs a complete overhaul. She'd like to open a hobby shop. "Not really to make money but to have some place to go each day."

Mrs. Becker and her sister in front of the renovated Medicine Valley School.

A desk from the old school is an antique treasure in Mrs. Becker's new home.

Jim Shock, 83, marvels at the strides man has taken in recent decades. "We've even seen a man on the moon," says the former cowboy.

OLD COWBOY

Jim and Mary Shock live in a comfortable home just off Tecumseh Road, 15 miles west of Toppenish. They have all the comforts of home — water, electricity, a range, a washer and a dryer and television for entertainment. When they want to go to town now, there is a car available which will be driven over paved roads. But... it has not always been such an easy life for them.

Jim, Sh-maw-yeah, was born in Priest Rapids in 1892. When his mother died, he came to the Valley. Here, he met Mary Wahwyser, who had lived in the area since her birth in 1902. They were married in 1923.

Jim remembers the days when he traveled by horseback to go here and there over dusty roads and trails. "There was sagebrush everywhere," recalls the former cowboy. In the spring, he would go with his mother over to the Soap Lake area to gather roots for food. In late summer, they would go up toward Gold Hill and Mt. Adams for huckleberries. They fished at Horn Rapids near Benton City and dried most of what they caught for winter.

Mary went to Fort Simcoe Indian boarding school for about three years. Jim never did go to school, but learned the language and how to write his name. Now, his eyesight is poor; and as he doesn't want to wear glasses, he thumb prints.

Jim's lack of formal education did not prevent him from becoming one of the top cowboys of his day. He broke horses that he rounded up in the mountains, and with his family trekked to Pendleton, Oregon, over 50 times to participate in their annual "Round-Up" days.

He trapped coyote, skunk, rabbits and muskrats for their furs which were needed in those days. He sold them to Al Wunch who used to run the Teepee Market on Fort Road.

Jim and Mary Shock have six children: Lillian Spino, Adams, Oregon; Marcella Miller, Wapato; Evelyn Andy, Brownstown; and Christine Billy, who with her husband, Cecil, live with and care for the parents. Two sons, Wesley and Sam, are deceased. All together there are 23 grandchildren and eleven great-grandchildren. When Jim and Mary were first married, they lived near "the Creek," but after their first child was born they moved the house further away.

Jim, in his 83 years, has only been in the hospital once. In the winter of 1965, he was hunting up in the mountains, and coming home on horseback his feet were frostbitten.

Because of an accident, Mary has been in a wheelchair for several years; but now she is beginning to walk with a cane. She spends much of her time making beautiful beaded bags, necklaces, and she recently made a dress for grand-daughter, Cynthia. When tules are available, she makes tule mats. While she is unable to dig roots any more, she cares for them when they are brought home to her.

The Shocks speak of their nice neighbor, Annie Braden to whom they used to give Indian roots. They remember the Braden boys. Jack, (a Benton Rural Electric board member), still lives nearby. "He is a good neighbor, too," Jim says.

When the Shocks celebrate their 52nd anniversary next month, they will probably recall with their family and friends, the horse and buggy days, the kerosene lamps, the hand pumps they used to get water... but no more... Benton Rural Electric has helped in so many ways.

As they sit in their secluded home surrounded by green lawns and flowers in the Valley they love, dominated by the big mountain to the west, they often reflect on the good things that have come to them. "We've even seen a man on the moon," says the small, weathered man, who is one of the last of the "old cowboys." His wife, Mary added "How things have changed!"

Mary Shock

Marjorie Pinkham, a Navaho, living on the Yakima Reservation shares her arts and crafts of the southwest with her friends here.

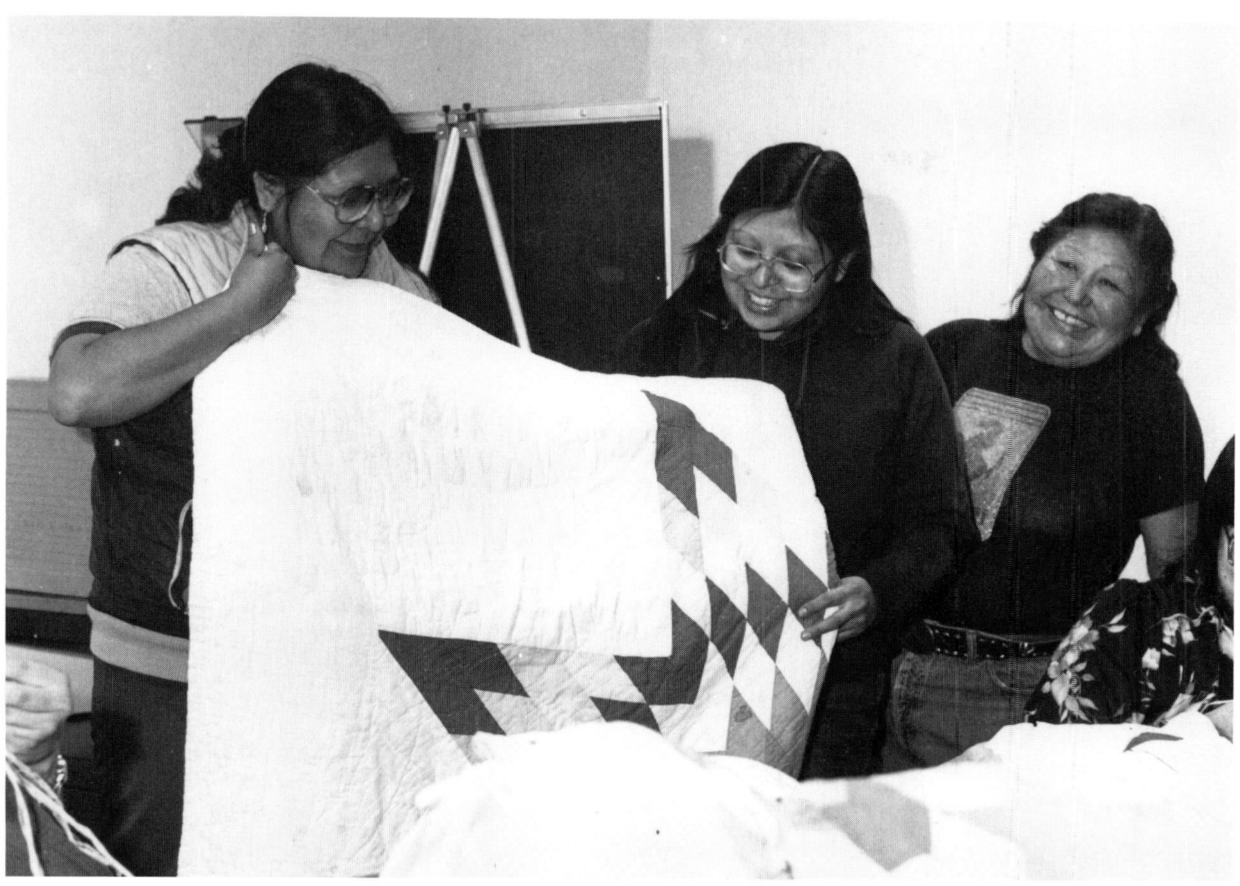

LIVING TRADITIONS!

They work with tiny stitches, cedar root, beads, silk and velvet, polyester and cotton yardage, manmade and natural materials.

They are members of the Yakima Indian Nation Extension Club.

Extension clubs associated with the County Extension Service have been around for years in rural and small-town areas. Members of these clubs study nutrition, clothing, interior decorating and landscaping — whatever the needs of a specific group may be — with a county extension agent trained in these various fields, to make their lives and their homes more pleasant.

The Yakima Indian Nation Extension Club members do this and much more. They include in their objectives retaining and sharing their cultural arts and crafts — especially bead work, basketry and dressmaking.

Some 20 members meet with coordinator Lucinda Bill every other Wednesday evening, 7 - 9:30, in the Yakima Indian Agency conference room on Fort Road near Toppenish. While business meetings are held as necessary, most of their time and effort goes into working on their individual projects.

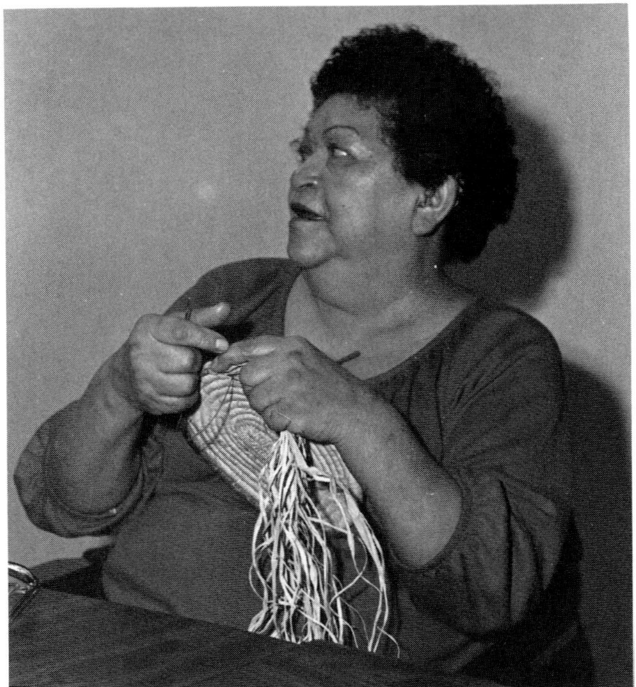

The young ones and the Old Ones alike put their best efforts into the beaded belts, purses, hair pieces, buckskin, cotton, silk or velvet wing dresses, buckskin moccasins, vests, hats, quilts, etcetera. Many loving stiches go into clothing made by mothers and grandmothers for the wee ones., the teenagers and for themselves, who will wear them proudly at ceremonials, family gatherings and pow-wows. Others make articles to sell, and these talented ladies have orders ahead all the time.

Many of the articles made last year were on exhibit at the Washington State Fair in Yakima last fall. "This year we are going to enter in the competition," states Lucinda.

Among those practicing the ancient art of basketry are Elsie Louis, Jo Anne Salatsee and Gloria Clark. Baskets were very important in the past. Used for root gathering, berry picking, for storage and even for cooking, they were made of Indian hemp, tule or cattails, fiber from cedar roots and cottonwood. Intricate designs were woven in with materials colored with dye from the Oregon grape, huckleberries, earth or other vegetable matter.

"Today we make them for gifts, to trade or sell or just to keep the art alive," says Elsie, who makes them of all sizes. Jo Anne specializes in the tiny ones. "Natural materials are hard to find, so most we buy." Gloria is the only one who is still using cedar root, which she and her friends find in the hills at a certain time in the fall. It must be cured and prepared by a lengthy process for future use in weaving.

Patience is necessary in all of the craft work. Working with tiny beads and following your own design is fun but time-consuming; but for those who enjoy it there is always time. Designs usually depict one's own thoughts about life, the earth, heavens, stars, moon, sun, animal. Marjorie Pinkham and Marcella Miller like the bead work.

There's an art to dressmaking, too. Styles change according to the tribe and times. The traditional wing dress may be of plain cotton, polyester or such. It may be adorned with ribbons or other materials. Dresses worn for ceremonials and pow-wows are elegant, of buckskin decorated with beads, shells, feathers, or they may be of rich velvet with the same adornments. Hours and hours of loving care go into the outfit, complete with buckskin moccasins and leggings, hairpieces, necklaces, shawls and purses. As the members work, they chat about everyday affairs or share their ideas.

Dance contests, queen contests and entertainments require the best. It is here that the talents of mothers and grandmothers are noticed, as often the dress is judged, along with several other criteria. Once these are completed they may be passed on from generation to generation — from aunt to niece, etcetera. Esther Speedis has chosen a plum-colored velvet for a granddaughter, which she will finish with shells and beads. It will be worn with pride.

Quiltmaking has also intrigued the ladies recently, notes Lucinda. They are preparing several for themselves, but will be shown at the fair first.

Some, like Sarah Zack, have numerous talents. She not only does bead work, basketry, crochets, hooks rugs, makes quilts and embroiders, but she teaches such at Seattle Indian Christian Mission. She is also a story teller and a whistler.

Marjorie Pinkham, a Navaho married to a Yakima, is versatile in arts and crafts. She share the traditions of her tribe, which lives in the Southwest.

The club is organized with Jo Anne Salatsee as president, Sheryl Antelope as vice president, Dorothy Everybody Talks-about as secretary and Margaret Root as treasurer.

The Yakima Indian Nation Extension Program is associated with the Yakima County Extension Service. Lucinda, an extension aide, has the responsibility of organizing and maintaining 4-H and Homemakers groups from Ellensburg to Celilo, Oregon. She is an enrolled Yakima, born in Toppenish, and has spent all of her 38 years in the area. She has had the opportunity to learn from the Old Ones, and now in her work wants to share with others to keep the traditions alive.

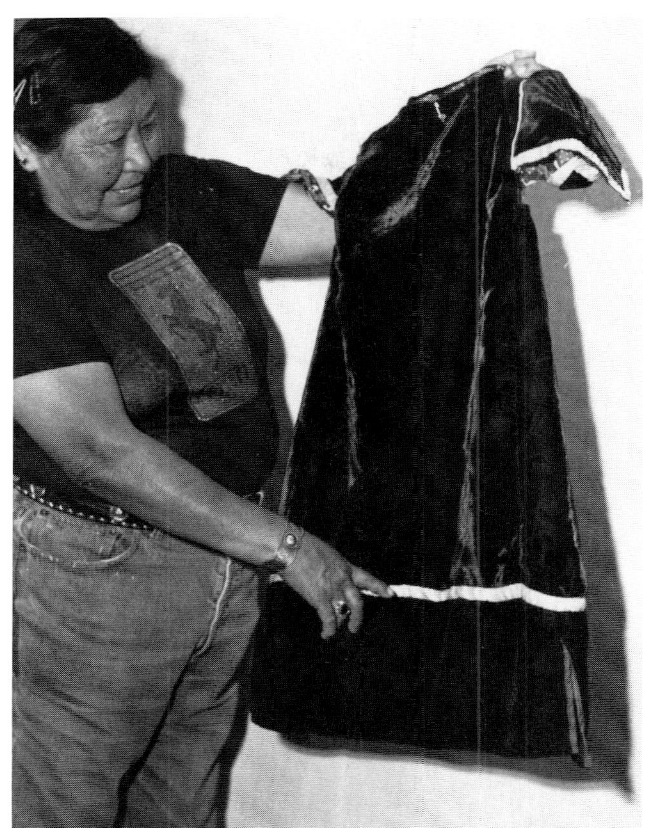

Grandmother is spending many hours fashioning this ribbon dress for her granddaughter. Clothing designs do change and little girls like to be dressed "just right."

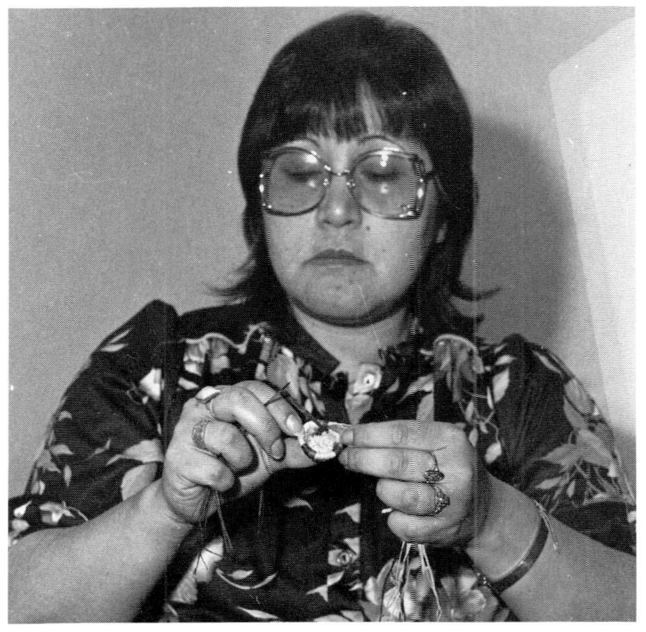

Jo Anne Salatsee starts a tiny basket. The Yakima Indians are known far and wide for their beautiful basketry.

Royalty leads out at the 1990 Toppenish Pow-wow, followed by family and friends. This event took place outdoors.

Guests at Spelly-mi join in for a social dance. Dress for the Indian dancers has become more elaborate in recent years. In fact, in early days, it was the warriors who danced the night before a big foray to give themselves a "pep talk."

Feathers, furs, beads and bangles adorn this regal lady. If she steps to the drum as well as she has chosen her costume she should be in line for a nice prize. It may take years to collect "just the right" articles for a dance dress.

Index

Q.

R.

S.

T.

U.

W.

Y.

Z.